MAX notes®

Sophocles'

The Oedipus Trilogy

Text by
Laurie Kahmanson
(M.A. Uni...

D0967343

Dr.
Chief Editor

Illustrations by
Michael A. Kupka

Research & Education Association

MAXnotes® for
THE OEDIPUS TRILOGY

Printed in the United States of America

Library of Congress Catalog Card Number 96-67439

International Standard Book Number 0-87891-036-0

MAXnotes® is a registered trademark of
Research & Education Association, Piscataway, New Jersey 08854

What **MAXnotes**® *Will Do for You*

This book is intended to help you absorb the essential contents and features of Sophocles' *The Oedipus Trilogy* and to help you gain a thorough understanding of the work. The book has been designed to do this more quickly and effectively than any other study guide.

For best results, this **MAXnotes** book should be used as a companion to the actual work, not instead of it. The interaction between the two will greatly benefit you.

To help you in your studies, this book presents the most up-to-date interpretations of every section of the actual work, followed by questions and fully explained answers that will enable you to analyze the material critically. The questions also will help you to test your understanding of the work and will prepare you for discussions and exams.

Meaningful illustrations are included to further enhance your understanding and enjoyment of the literary work. The illustrations are designed to place you into the mood and spirit of the work's settings.

The **MAXnotes** also include summaries, character lists, explanations of plot, and section-by-section analyses. A biography of the author and discussion of the work's historical context will help you put this literary piece into the proper perspective of what is taking place.

The use of this study guide will save you the hours of preparation time that would ordinarily be required to arrive at a complete grasp of this work of literature. You will be well prepared for classroom discussions, homework, and exams. The guidelines that are included for writing papers and reports on various topics will prepare you for any added work which may be assigned.

The **MAXnotes** will take your grades "to the max."

Dr. Max Fogiel
Program Director

Contents

**Each section includes List of Characters,
Summary, Analysis, Study Questions and
Answers, and Suggested Essay Topics.**

Introduction

The Life and Work of Sophocles

Although records from the ancient world are fragmentary, Sophocles is generally credited with authorship of more than 100 plays, including *Oedipus the King, Oedipus at Colonus* and *Antigone.* These three plays, known as *The Oedipus Trilogy,* were written separately, but they are often read and studied together. The order in which they are generally studied is *Oedipus the King, Oedipus at Colonus* and *Antigone,* but the third play was written and performed first.

Only a small fraction of the work credited to Sophocles survives, including the three complete plays discussed here, four other complete plays, and fragments of about 100 other works.

Standard biographies of Sophocles agree that he was born in the year 496 B.C., in Colonus, and lived to be 90 years old. Raised in a wealthy family, he was well educated for his time and enjoyed all the advantages of his social status. His family's connections, combined with the prestige he earned as a public figure and as a playwright, won him honor and fame during his lifetime. Then and now, Sophocles ranked as one of the leading dramatists of the ancient world. His work is studied today for its tragic power, its dramatic strengths and its human richness.

Sophocles first became known as a leading author of the Greek theater when he defeated the reigning playwright, Aeschylus, in a public contest in 468 B.C. The public playwriting contests were the ancient cultural equivalent of our Academy Awards, Tony Awards and Pulitzer Prize all rolled into one.

Sophocles went on to win 20 first-place prizes in Athenian drama competitions, making him a leading cultural figure of his time. The theater of the ancient world grew out of religious festivals, and the surviving scripts have a liturgical elegance and formality. The plays of Sophocles are firmly rooted in the formal traditions of his era.

The main themes of the plays Sophocles wrote—human strength, human weakness, divine power and divine will, fate and free will—are still important in modern literature and popular culture. The spectacle of a hugely gifted yet greatly flawed human being struggling to do the right thing is still as theatrically powerful now as it was when Sophocles crafted his versions of the timeless human story. Whether the tragically flawed heroes of modern entertainment make their stands in the arenas of politics, science fiction or opera, the mighty are still brought low by hubris, or pride, and fate is still inescapable.

There is one major difference between ancient entertainment and the popular culture we consume today. That difference is not Hollywood's wondrous technology; what's different is the scripts. From movies to television sit-coms, today's dramas typically have happy endings. It was not always thus.

Sophocles worked from the premise that the mechanisms of drama must inexorably deliver characters to destruction. The inevitability of the journey was what made it tragic.

Watching these tragedies build toward their inescapable conclusions, audiences experienced powerful, primal emotions—grief, pity and fear—in the controlled setting of the theater. What they got from the experience was the ritualistic purification and release called catharsis of emotion.

Historical Background

The long life that Sophocles lived touched the centuries when the arc of Athenian civilization rose and fell sharply. Athens had been a contested corner of the globe since the time of the Old Testament's kings. Many centuries of war and tyranny, illuminated by brief flashes of democratic reforms, shaped the history of the city-state into which Sophocles was born. The city felt the lash of tyranny again in the years after Sophocles died.

During the 5th century B.C., when Sophocles wrote, the political theory underpinning our own democracy was taking form in Athens. But this theory, and its democratic ideals of freedom and justice that inspire us today, applied to only a fraction of the people living in Athens during the playwright's lifetime.

The rights, responsibilities and freedoms of citizenship in the Athens that Sophocles entertained with his art were available only to a small, elite class of men. Women of any class—slave or free—were denied what we think of today as basic rights. The legions of slaves that performed the society's hardest labor—women and men—were denied liberty, the most fundamental of all democratic rights.

Despite the flawed application of democratic theory in ancient Greece, the ideals developed then and there shaped the modern world's principles of human rights, responsibilities and freedoms. By the 19th century, the inspirations that American intellectuals and political leaders drew from ancient Greece could be seen and touched in towns and cities across this country.

Reproduced on thousands of courthouses, libraries and other public buildings, the Greek Revival style of architecture combined admiration of the past with modern copies of the columns and pediments of ancient Athens. These buildings often had proclamations of liberty, justice and freedom carved into the marble slabs above their entrances.

Many of the Greek Revival buildings specifically echo the shape and structure of the Parthenon—a temple to Athena, the goddess of wisdom, that was built as a public works project while Sophocles lived. Generally considered to be the greatest masterpiece of Greek architecture, the Parthenon stands on the Acropolis, overlooking Athens.

The leader of Athens during the years when Sophocles lived was Pericles, and the Age of Pericles gave the world architecture, comedies, tragedies and political ideas that are still studied today.

In later centuries, Athens suffered more wars and a mix of defeats and victories, but no conqueror erased its status as a place where art and philosophy were nurtured.

The three plays discussed here are typical of ancient Greek drama and philosophy. Themes of determination and pride—or hubris—inevitably leading characters to destinies they urgently try to avoid were common.

These plays have been performed for thousands of years—in ancient, open-air theaters seating as many people as modern sports arenas, and in revival houses seating only a few hundred patrons. The ancient Greek theater was highly stylized and formal, and the plays were constructed formulaically, with clear beginnings, middles and ends. There is some debate about the exact layout and structure of the performance spaces, but there is general agreement about the rough outlines.

The Greek theaters seated about 20,000 people in a steeply sloping semi-circle whose straight edge was the stage. The actors worked in clearly defined spaces. The Chorus delivered its verses from a flat, low area close to the audience. The other performers spoke from a raised platform set behind the choral space.

While the characters went about fighting their destinies, many missing pieces of background, characterization and plot were supplied to the audience by the chorus.

The function of the Greek chorus survives in modern popular culture in the form of the sidekicks in television shows and movies who speak to the audience as much as they do to other characters. This device serves now, as it did in the ancient world, to move the plot along, deepen characterization, and tell the audience more than is being said by the other characters.

Master List of Characters

Oedipus the King

Oedipus—*The King of Thebes, who is unknowingly married to his mother, Jocasta.*

Priest—*A priest of Zeus, king of the gods.*

Creon—*The brother of Jocasta.*

Chorus—*A group of Theban elders and their Leader, whose commentary helps the audience understand the events on stage.*

Tiresias—*The blind prophet who sees the future.*

Jocasta—*The Queen of Thebes, who is married to Oedipus, her son, but doesn't know it.*

A Messenger—*A messenger who delivers news.*

A Shepherd—*The shepherd saves Oedipus, when, as a baby, he is abandoned with his feet bound on a barren mountainside.*

A Messenger—*This messenger from the palace sees a grim sight.*

Antigone—*The daughter of Oedipus and Jocasta.*

Ismene—*Antigone's sister.*

Oedipus at Colonus
Oedipus—*The former King of Thebes.*

Antigone—*The daughter of Oedipus, the former king, and his queen, also his mother.*

A Citizen—*A citizen or free man of Colonus.*

Chorus—*A group of elders from Colonus and their Leader, whose commentary helps the audience understand the events on stage*

Ismene—*The daughter of Oedipus, the former king, and his queen, also his mother.*

Theseus—*The King of Athens, which includes Colonus.*

Creon—*The King of Thebes, and brother of Jocasta.*

Polynices—*The son of Oedipus, and Jocasta. His sisters are Ismene and Antigone.*

A Messenger—*A messenger who delivers news.*

Antigone
Antigone—*The daughter of Oedipus and Jocasta.*

Ismene—*Antigone's sister.*

Chorus—*A group of Theban elders and their Leader, whose commentary helps the audience understand the events on stage.*

Creon—*The King of Thebes, and the uncle of Antigone and Ismene.*

A Sentry—*A soldier.*

Haemon—*The son of King Creon and Eurydice, he is Antigone's lover.*

Tiresias—*The blind prophet who sees the future.*

A Messenger—*A man who delivers grim news.*

Eurydice—*The wife of King Creon, and the mother of Haemon.*

Summary of the Plays

The three plays can be studied together or individually. Each is complete in itself, and ancient audiences knew the rough outlines of the plot from long oral traditions that preceded formal theatrical productions of these stories.

Antigone flowed first from Sophocles' hand, and was seen first by ancient audiences, but it comes last in the lives of the characters, wrapping up the final disasters of their histories.

The first play in the characters' lives is *Oedipus the King*, which is the story of a man unwittingly moving ever closer to the unhappy fate he is struggling mightily to avoid.

The child Oedipus is born to the royal couple, Laius and Jocasta, but a grim prophecy hangs over the Theban palace. The old king is warned that his son will kill him. In order to thwart fate, Laius and Jocasta abandon the infant Oedipus, with his feet bound, to starve on a barren mountainside.

Rescued by the shepherd who was supposed to leave the baby to starve, and delivered to the royal palace at Corinth by a Messenger, Oedipus is raised as the son of the royal house. Life there is good, until Oedipus learns that a prophecy has named him as the murderer of his father and the husband of his mother. Determined to outwit fate, the young man flees the only home—and the only father—he has known.

Soon, the wandering Oedipus meets and kills a stranger at a crossroads, and part of the oracle's prophecy is fulfilled. Oedipus doesn't know it, but the murdered stranger is Laius, his real father. The wanderer has committed one of the very acts he fled Corinth to avoid.

Continuing his journey, Oedipus enters Thebes—his forgotten first home—as a hero, having solved the riddle of the murderous Sphinx. The evil creature murdered travelers who could not solve its riddle; "What goes on four legs in the morning, two legs in the afternoon and three legs at night?" Oedipus is the first person to figure out the answer: As crawling infants, people travel on four limbs in the mornings of their lives. As adults, they travel upright on two limbs in the bright middays of their lives. As frail and elderly people tapping canes before them, they travel on three limbs in the twilights of their days.

Oedipus' reward for solving the riddle is marriage to Jocasta, the Queen of Thebes. She is the widow of the recently murdered king, Laius, whose slaying is an unsolved crime at the time. Unfortunately, Jocasta doesn't recognize Oedipus as her abandoned son, and this ill-fated marriage goes forward.

This much of the plot is background, which is revealed in pieces later in the story. The history was well-known to ancient Greek audiences, and the story was part of their canon of stories and legends.

The action of *Oedipus the King* begins during a time of plague in Thebes. The gods demand vengeance for the death of Laius as the price of lifting the city's punishment. Oedipus, who has been a wise and just ruler of the people who made him their king, is determined to seek justice. Through his efforts, he discovers that he is the murderer of Laius.

Before this search for the truth is complete, Jocasta figures out the secret and kills herself. When he discovers her body, Oedipus puts out his own eyes. The play closes with Oedipus mourning the destruction of his family, apologizing to his daughters, and begging Creon, the new king and Jocasta's brother, for banishment. His wish is granted. The girls become their uncle Creon's wards, but their ill-fated brothers are left to look out for themselves.

The storyline continues in *Oedipus at Colonus*, which features the blind former king as a shattered old man. His daughter, Antigone, is his loyal companion. Wandering together, they come upon a sacred grove that is protected by the Furies, who are also known as the Eumenides—the protectors of Athens.

When he discovers where he is, Oedipus realizes that the last piece of the prophecy foretelling his life is about to be fulfilled. If he is granted shelter there and dies there, on Athenian soil, his body will draw the blood of the enemy—in this case, the invading force of Thebes, his former home.

Before that happens, other curses and prophesies are cast and fulfilled. Back home in Thebes, his two sons are quarreling over the throne Oedipus abandoned, and one comes to him seeking help. Oedipus greets his son, Polynices, with the curse of mutual fratricidal murder.

When the play ends, that curse has been fulfilled. Polynices and Eteocles have killed each other in battle. The final tragedy of the family cycle will unwind in *Antigone*, when their doomed sister meets her own fate.

Antigone, the play that wraps together the final events of these characters' sad lives, begins in Thebes. After her father's death, Antigone has returned to the royal palace where she was raised. Her family's tragedies have been compounded by her brothers Eteocles and Polynices, who have killed each other in war, as foretold by their father.

The ruling king, Creon, gives an honorable burial to one of his nephews, Eteocles, but there is no such mercy for Polynices. Declaring him a traitor, Creon forbids burial of his corpse and promises death to anyone who disobeys this order.

Grief-stricken and defiant, Antigone performs burial rites for her brother, saying that the gods demand no less of her. Her sister, Ismene, tries to prevent yet another tragedy, without success. Creon upholds his decree, and condemns Antigone to be buried alive. Creon later rescinds this order, but his second thoughts come too late. Antigone has already committed suicide by the time Creon changes his mind and decides that sentencing her to death was wrong. Haemon, her lover, who is Creon's son, takes his own life when he discovers that he can only join his would-be bride in the kingdom of the dead.

The destruction of the two royal families is now concluded.

Estimated Reading Time

The three plays are not very long, but they are written in detailed prose that demands and rewards careful attention. Each play can be read in about three hours.

The reading sessions are best broken up into intervals of about 40 minutes. By following the line-and-section markings in this MAX*notes* guide, the student can absorb each play in logically divided portions. Each portion ends with review questions and answers to help you gauge your understanding, plus essay questions.

SECTION TWO

Oedipus the King

Lines 1 – 525

New Characters:

Oedipus: *the King of Thebes, who is married to Jocasta, his mother*

Priest: *a priest of Zeus, the king of the gods*

Creon: *the brother of Jocasta, the mother of Oedipus*

Chorus: *a group of Theban elders and their Leader, whose commentary helps the audience understand the events on stage*

Tiresias: *the blind prophet who sees the future*

Summary

The play opens during the plague years in Thebes. Miserable and dying, the people don't know what to do about their condition. Nothing—not even prayers to the gods—is helping.

Oedipus is a great and kind king, and he feels the pain of his people. Approaching the faithful but despairing worshippers at his altar, he asks what he can do. A priest of Zeus, the king of all the gods, details the despair of the people. Death is everywhere. Crops, livestock, people—all are being stricken. Despite the devastation, the priest still has faith in the gods and in his king, and having made offerings at the altar he now begs Oedipus to do something.

The king says that he has already done something—he has sent his brother-in-law, Creon, to the Oracle at Delphi for advice. As omnipresent in ancient Greek affairs of state as political pundits

are today, the Oracle at Delphi combined the role of a religious shrine with that of a modern-day spin doctor. The Oracle's pronouncements were taken seriously by many powerful people, and it is a sign of humility and of respect for the gods that Oedipus sends for its advice.

Creon returns, and Oedipus immediately asks for news. Creon hints that it would best be delivered in private, but Oedipus insists on having Creon tell his news publicly. The news seems simple enough, at first. The Oracle has said that the murder of the previous king, Laius, must be avenged.

The complicated part is how to do this. The crime has gone unsolved for many years, and any clues the murderer left have long since disappeared. Oedipus mocks the people for having let such a crime go unsolved and unpunished. He vows to find the killer, serve justice and stop the plague.

In a long speech, the Chorus mourns the dead, and begs the gods for help.

Oedipus hears the fervent prayers, and tells the Chorus to look to him for deliverance. He announces his intention to find and punish whoever killed Laius, and he warns of terrible punishments for anyone who hides the truth.

The Leader of the Chorus suggests that the blind prophet Tiresias might be able to help, and the ever-vigilant Oedipus says a message has already been sent to him. This is an early foreshadowing of the interplay between sight and blindness that builds throughout the play. It is one of the play's central ironies that the blind old man is the first to see the truth.

For all his strength, intelligence and wisdom, Oedipus is blind to the central and most tragic facts of his life—that he is the man who murdered his father and that he has taken his mother as his wife. Although he has constructed his life to avoid the fate that was foretold for him, he has failed to see that all his efforts have only led him closer to fulfulling that grim prophecy.

When the Leader sees Tiresias coming, he announces that the prophet is the man who will convict the old king's murderer. He speaks more profoundly than he knows.

Oedipus welcomes the prophet, with praise for his powers and his knowledge. But the seer is strangely reticent. He wishes only to go back home, without speaking.

At first cajolingly and then angrily, Oedipus insists on hearing what Tiresias has to say. Tiresias says that Oedipus is the cause of the plagues, and that the king is the murderer. In a rage, Oedipus rejects Tiresias and his vision, and accuses the seer of conspiring with Creon against the throne.

The Leader of the Chorus tries to smooth over the situation, but it's too late. Tiresias answers Oedipus furiously, saying that the king can see far less than a blind man can. The section ends with mutual threats and insults.

Analysis

This storyline and its characters were part of ancient Greece's oral traditions long before the first performance of this play, and the audience knew exactly what would happen before the gears of the plot begin turning. But the relentless, clockwork motion of the play kept theatergoers rapt then, as it does now, because watching fate unfold when it is known to you but not to the people who are its prisoners is a privilege borrowed from the gods.

The Greek audiences who attended performances knew that Oedipus is bold, mighty, and just, he has human temper tantrums and he is doomed. Their world view included the idea that brave, wise, clever heroes who were tragically flawed by out-of-control pride—hubris—would inevitably be destroyed. That idea is a central theme of *Oedipus the King*.

Before the action of this play begins, Oedipus has already attempted to outrun fate, marking himself early for destruction. By attempting to escape a prophecy that he would kill his father, and leaving the palace at Corinth where he was raised, he sets the machinery of doom in motion.

Traveling along the highways, he soon enough meets and murders a man he thinks is merely an overly aggressive stranger. Years later, he discovers that the dead man is his natural father, Laius, and that he has unwittingly performed the act he was trying to avoid. The audiences of the ancient world knew all this when they filed into the outdoor, stone theaters where the play was staged.

The play begins with Oedipus again attempting to reshape the arc of his life that was described by prophecy. The hints of his coming failure are numerous.

In the Priest's first long speech, when he begs Oedipus to save the city, he appeals to the king's long experience—as a statesman, as a wanderer, as a ruler and as a vagrant. Unknown to the Priest and to Oedipus—but known to the audience—is that this king's experience also includes killing his father and marrying his mother. The very experience to which the Priest appeals is moving Oedipus step by step to destruction.

This exchange between the Priest and Oedipus is but one example of how Sophocles built dramatic tension into his play by including multiple levels of meaning in a single statement.

The technique will be repeated throughout the play. It reappears just a few lines later, when Oedipus tells the Priest that he has asked for help from the Oracle at Delphi and will follow its advice or consider himself a traitor. With the borrowed omniscience of the gods, the audience knows that Oedipus is already a traitor for having killed Laius, and that he will be faced with pronouncing the judgment he has pronounced upon himself. It remains only to witness what happens.

In another exchange weighted with similarly complex levels of meaning, Creon tells Oedipus what he has learned from the Oracle. Creon begins with the murder of Laius as background, and Oedipus says that he knows of the previous king, but has never seen him. Creon continues, delivering the Oracle's instructions, and Oedipus vows to find and punish the murderer of Laius.

While the Oracle's wishes are being delivered by Creon and while Oedipus reacts to them, the audience knows, as before, what Oedipus does not—that he murdered Laius, that he is the dead king's son and that the widowed queen Oedipus married is his mother.

Once again, there is something transfixing, tragic and doomed about watching Oedipus, in his ignorance, attempting to follow the Oracle's orders but all the time preparing for the revelation of his crime and his subsequent doom.

The first hint of the truth is revealed to Oedipus by the blind prophet, Tiresias, and the king answers the seemingly unbelievable charge with rage, insults and threats. Raised in Corinth by the royal house as if he were the natural son of his adoptive parents, Oedipus rejects what Tiresias says as errant nonsense. The blind prophet, who taunts Oedipus as being the one who is unable to see the truth—has challenged the king to reconsider everything about himself—his parentage, his childhood and how he came to rule Thebes and marry the city's widowed queen. The challenge is met with rage, and Oedipus ends this section unable to see the truth or to hear well-intentioned advice.

Study Questions

1. What is the condition of the people of Thebes when the play opens?

2. What is Creon's relationship to Oedipus?

3. What is the meaning of the long prayer by the Chorus?

4. How does Oedipus respond to the long prayer by the Chorus?

5. What curse does Oedipus call down on the murderer of Laius?

6. What does Oedipus ask Tiresias to do when the seer arrives?

7. How does Tiresias first respond?

8. Why does Tiresias respond the way he does?

9. How does Oedipus change in his dealings with Tiresias?

10 What is the meaning of what Tiresias reveals?

Answers

1. When the play opens, the people of Thebes are sick, weak and dying. Their crops are blighted and there is a plague on the land.

2. Creon is the brother of Jocasta, the widowed queen of Thebes who married Oedipus. Along with being the brother-in-law of Oedipus, Creon is his uncle, because Oedipus is Jocasta's son.

3. The long prayer by the Chorus invokes several of the gods worshipped by the ancient Greeks and asks them to help Thebes in their specialized ways. The prayer shows the devotion of the Chorus to a religion that was being challenged in rationalist intellectual circles.

4. In his response to the long prayer by the Chorus, Oedipus reveals himself as one who believes he is beyond the power of the gods. When he tells the people of Thebes to look to him for answers, he usurps the role of the gods in human affairs.

5. Oedipus curses the murderer of Laius with a life that is agony. He calls down a further list, including barren fields, infertility, and death to sons who are already born.

6. When the seer Tiresias arrives, Oedipus tells him that the Oracle requires justice for Laius and asks the prophet to rescue the city.

7. Tiresias first responds by saying that it is terrible to see the truth, as he does, because it brings only pain. He asks to be sent home.

8. Tiresias responds the way he does because he knows the truth and dreads the destruction it will bring if he reveals it.

9. Oedipus changes in his dealings with Tiresias from friend and patron to a hurler of insults, threats and accusations of envy and extortion.

10. On one level, the blind prophet's revelation simply states the facts known to nobody but him. On the metaphorical level, the blind old man is presented as the person whose sight is more accurate than the king's.

Suggested Essay Topics

1. The gods are a strong presence in this play, invoked by many characters for many reasons. Discuss the role the gods play in human life—as healers, as bearers of prophecy, as beings that must be appeased and as forces shaping fate and destiny.

2. The underlying theme of this play is the question of free will and how human beings shape their own lives. Do you believe that we are destined to fulfill some role already scripted for us? Do you believe that you are free to shape your own life? Do you believe that human actions can have effects and consequences that are only known much later?

Lines 526 – 1,165

New Characters:

Jocasta: *the Queen of Thebes, who is married to her son, Oedipus*

A Messenger: *a messenger from Corinth*

Summary

This section begins with a long song from the Chorus, whose faith in the power of prophecy and in Oedipus, their King, is being sorely tested. One thing is certain—that someone who committed the terrible crime of murdering Laius is loose in the city, and fate lies in wait to punish him, the Chorus says. But the prophet Tiresias, who has always been reliable, is now making terrible accusations against a king who has been brave, just and wise, casting the Chorus into turmoil. Deciding to put off any decision, the Chorus demands proof before accepting the charges Tiresias has made.

The gods, who know the truth, could supply the truth the Chorus seeks, but Zeus and Apollo are keeping what they know to themselves. While the Chorus waits for the gods to speak, the members hope that Oedipus turns out to be innocent.

Creon enters then, proclaiming his innocence. Angry and feeling wronged, he wants to confront his brother-in-law over the charges of conspiracy and treason that Oedipus has publicly hurled at him and Tiresias. The Leader of the Chorus advises calm, saying Creon should consider overlooking the incident. But that is not going to happen, because Oedipus enters and repeats the charge.

The two men interrogate each other, trying to prove guilt and innocence, and Creon cleverly argues that he doesn't want the throne. Being the king's brother-in-law gives Creon all the prestige and wealth of the ruler with none of his responsibilities, Creon says. The Leader of the Chorus hears reason in what Creon says, and suggests that Oedipus is being hasty in condemning his relative. Oedipus rejects this advice, saying he wants Creon dead. The two men resume their argument, and the Leader of the Chorus attempts to intervene when Jocasta enters.

Jocasta is Creon's sister and the wife of Oedipus, and she breaks up the fight between them by shaming them into silence. She gets from each man a brief version of his side of the story, and then she asks Oedipus to believe her brother's denials and to spare his life. The Chorus sides with Jocasta and Creon, and says that Oedipus would do well not to execute a kinsman on a whim. Oedipus yields, but without grace. Creon leaves, muttering prophetically that Oedipus is the type of man who goes too far. Oedipus and Jocasta quarrel over Creon, and the Chorus interrupts them, saying there is trouble enough in Thebes without the royal couple fighting and making things worse.

The Chorus gives Oedipus and Jocasta some privacy, and the Queen asks the King why he is so upset. Oedipus says that Creon has schemed with Tiresias to pin the murder of Laius on him.

Trying to calm her husband, Jocasta says that she and Laius long ago outwitted the gods and their prophets, and that he need not fear them either. Proclaiming victory over everything sacred, Jocasta tells Oedipus how she and her first husband, Laius, cheated fate. It was prophesied that their son would kill his father, and Jocasta and Laius undid that foretelling by abandoning their infant boy to starve on a mountainside Everything turned out fine, Jocasta says, and there's nothing to worry about now.

Instead of calming Oedipus, his wife's narrative makes him more upset. Pieces of memory begin forming themselves into frightening shapes in his mind. As he quizzes Jocasta on the details of the former king's murder that filtered back to the palace, Oedipus begins to suspect that he murdered Laius. Jocasta tells Oedipus not to jump to conclusions, and they agree to send for the old, freed slave who is the murder's sole surviving witness.

Oedipus then delivers a long, soul-searching speech. He still believes himself to be the son of the Corinthian king, Polybus, but he is bothered by a dim memory of a drunken reveler at a banquet saying otherwise. At the time, his parents denied that he was adopted, and he believed them.

He continues his history with the story of his visit to the Oracle at Delphi, where he heard for himself the prophecy that he would kill his father and wed his mother. A loving son to the only parents he has ever known, and a bold and intelligent man who believes he can use his powers to thwart fate, Oedipus fled and never returned.

Wandering, Oedipus soon meets and kills an old man and the escorts accompanying him. The confrontation begins as an ordinary roadside fight over who has the right-of-way, but it escalates quickly into murder. The old man started the fight, according to the version of events that Oedipus remembers. By nearly running Oedipus off the road—and then striking him—the old man asked for a fight. But what the old man got was death, and the fulfillment of the prophecy that he would be killed by his son. Oedipus is just beginning to figure out who the old man was. Telling the story, Oedipus feels his memories connect now with the present, and he sees for the first time that he killed the stranger at the same crossroads where Laius was murdered.

Showing humility for the first time in many scenes, Oedipus prays to the gods that someone can somehow clear him of the crime he now suspects he committed.

Jocasta answers by telling Oedipus to put his faith in her. Just as she and her first husband thwarted fate when they abandoned their infant son, so Oedipus outran his destiny when he fled Corinth.

Not exactly, says the Chorus, calling down the judgment of the gods. Furious at the prideful way in which Oedipus and Jocasta have proclaimed themselves to be capable of outsmarting the gods, the Chorus says that its members will worship the gods no more if the prophecy goes unfulfilled.

Jocasta herself soon has second thoughts about mocking the gods, and she prays to Apollo. Oedipus is distraught, and Jocasta says she feels helpless.

A Messenger from Corinth appears. He announces that Polybus, the King of Corinth is dead, and that the people want Oedipus to be their king. Hearing this, Oedipus believes that he is now free of at least part of the prophecy. If death has claimed his father, Polybus, then Oedipus cannot possibly commit patricide. He announces his victory over oracles and prophecy, and Jocasta shares his pride in thwarting fate.

This victory turns out to be illusory. Worried about the part of the prophecy that says he will marry his mother, Oedipus says he must stay away from Corinth as long as she is alive and well there. Attempting to comfort Oedipus, the Messenger from Corinth speaks and winds up revealing shattering details of the truth.

King Polybus raised Oedipus as his own son, the Messenger says, and Queen Merope loved the child as well as any natural mother, but they were only foster parents. Oedipus is free to go back to Corinth anytime he likes without fear of illicit relations with his mother, because Merope is no blood relation of his, the Messenger says.

Instead of bringing relief to Oedipus, this news increases his distress. He presses the Messenger for details, and the Messenger says that the child raised by Polybus and Merope was a foundling, rescued from a hillside where he was abandoned to starvation, his ankles bound together. A shepherd found the child and delivered it to the Messenger, who turned it over to the childless royal couple at the palace.

Oedipus asks for a description of the shepherd, and the Messenger says he remembers only that the man was a servant of Laius. Determined to know the whole story, Oedipus asks if anyone in the Chorus knows this shepherd.

The Leader of the Chorus says that's up to Jocasta to say.

Jocasta is beginning to suspect the truth—that the baby she abandoned not only killed Laius but is now her husband. She begs Oedipus to call off this quest.

Analysis

Several themes presented earlier in the play are built upon in this section—how pride and faith in his own abilities moves Oedipus ever onward toward doom, how a failure to honor the gods results in the very destruction they foretell, and how humanity is unable to escape what is predicted for it. The long speech by the Chorus that opens this section is a meditation on these themes, mixed with the confusion of loyal subjects who have been given some reason to doubt the king they revere above all mortals.

The argument between Creon and Oedipus that follows this speech underlines the human frailties of both—the brother-in-law whose defense against treason is his claim that he would be loathe to sacrifice the ease and comfort of his lifestyle as hanger-on for the responsibilities of power, and the king whose raging temper leads him to recommend execution on a whim. Neither man behaves well, and it takes Jocasta to end the argument.

Jocasta herself is a flawed individual. Her arrogant dismissal of the gods and her proclamations of victory over fate foretell her undoing. As much as Oedipus, she is unable to see until it is too late that her life fulfilled the very prophecy she sought vainly and pridefully to undo. Oedipus begins to see, in brief glimpses, how blind he has been to the central facts of his own life. He gets a clue when the Messenger from Corinth arrives. The Messenger comes to deliver news that is sad—the death of Polybus, the King of Corinth—but Oedipus takes joy in the idea that he has now evaded fate. You can't kill a dead man, Oedipus reasons, and now that Polybus has expired due to natural causes, Oedipus thinks himself free at last of the prophecy of patricide. His only problem now is to avoid marrying his mother. If he stays away from Corinth and steers clear of Queen Merope, the widowed queen, he will have outwitted fate completely.

Thinking that he is doing a good deed, the Messenger tells Oedipus that Queen Merope, the widow of Polybus, is no blood relation. It's fine for Oedipus to come back to Corinth any time—he's in no danger of fulfilling the prophecy there, the Messenger says. By telling Oedipus that the queen who raised him is not his natural mother, the Messenger has unknowingly revealed enough of the truth to make Oedipus tragically curious and to push Jocasta toward despair.

Motivated by a simple desire to ease worry, the Messenger has released the machineries of fate that will produce the full revelation of the truth and all its awful effects. His intentions were good, but the results will be very, very bad.

When the Messenger speaks, he is as blindly ignorant of his fatal role in serving destiny as Oedipus and Jocasta are of theirs. He speaks, but he does not see.

In this section, the theme is hammered home time and again that people go through their lives thinking they are fulfilling one purpose when they are actually lurching toward the completion of several others. The gods know this and watch events unfold from above. The first audiences of this play knew the histories of its characters before the first lines were spoken, and the drama unfolded for viewers who watched with the borrowed omniscience of the gods. Modern readers are left to decide for themselves what they think about fate, prophecy and human attempts to outrun destiny.

Study Questions

1. Who does the Chorus seek in the first long speech of this section?

2. What are the family relationships of Creon, Oedipus and Jocasta?

3. How does Creon react to the charges Oedipus has made against him?

4. Why does Oedipus spare Creon's life?

5. How does Creon react to being spared?

6. What is the family relationship of Jocasta, Laius and Oedipus?

7. How does Jocasta view prophecy, fate and the gods?

8. What news does the Messenger from Corinth bring?

9. What are the unexpected effects of this news?

10. Why does Jocasta beg Oedipus to stop his search for the shepherd the Messenger mentions?

Answers

1. The doomed man the Chorus seeks is the man who killed Laius. That man is Oedipus, but the Chorus doesn't believe that yet.

2. Creon is Jocasta's brother, which makes him the brother-in-law of Oedipus. He later finds out that he is also the uncle of Oedipus when he finds out that Oedipus is Jocasta's son.

3. Creon reacts to the charges Oedipus has made against him by arguing that it is not only bad and wrong to plot against a king, but that it doesn't make sense for a hanger-on at the palace to give up an easy life for the burden of wearing the crown.

4. Oedipus spares Creon's life because he is shamed by the Chorus and by Jocasta.

5. Creon reacts to being spared by uttering the prophetic words that Oedipus is a man who goes too far.

6. Jocasta is the widow of King Laius, with whom she abandoned her infant son, Oedipus. That infant grew to manhood in the palace at Corinth. He fled Corinth, wandered to Thebes, and married Jocasta.

7. Jocasta views prophecy, fate and the gods as challenges to her sovereignty, and she tries to thwart their will.

8. The news that the Messenger from Corinth brings is that the people want Oedipus to take the throne now that Polybus, the King, is dead.

9. There are several unexpected effects of this news. One is that the Messenger reveals that Oedipus was raised at the palace after he was abandoned by his natural parents and rescued by a shepherd. Another effect is that Jocasta begins to suspect that the infant she abandoned has grown to be the man who is her husband.

10. Jocasta begs Oedipus to stop his search for the shepherd who rescued the baby she and Laius abandoned. She fears what will happen if her suspicions turn out to be true. She is attempting again to thwart fate.

Suggested Essay Topics

1. The Chorus says that its faith in the gods will be shattered unless the prophecies it has heard come true. This seems to be a rather extreme statement. Discuss.

2. Jocasta's plea to Oedipus asking him to stop the search for the shepherd can be looked at in many ways. She is trying to protect herself and her family, but she is also attempting to block fate by diverting Oedipus from a search that could lead to disaster for him, herself and their city. What would you do in her situation?

3. The Messenger comes thinking that he is delivering a simple piece of news, and unwittingly sets in motion the fall of the House of Oedipus. Write a diary entry for that day from his point of view.

Lines 1,166 – 1,680

New Characters:

A Shepherd: *the shepherd saves Oedipus, when, as a baby he is abandoned with his feet bound on a barren mountainside*

A Messenger: *the messenger from the palace sees a grim sight*

Antigone: *the daughter of Oedipus and Jocasta, who are mother and son*

Ismene: *Antigone's sister*

Summary

Jocasta asks Oedipus to drop the idea of locating the shepherd who saved him from abandonment, but he won't hear of it. As deaf to her pleas as he is blind to the truth about himself, he vows to discover his origins. Leaving the stage with a cry of anguished grief, Jocasta worries the Leader of the Chorus, who suggests to Oedipus that the Queen's sorrow could lead to something awful. He's right, as the play's earliest audiences knew, but Oedipus brushes off the Leader's concerns. Vowing to discover his origins, Oedipus once again displays his unerring ability to walk into trouble by acting on his passion.

Trouble appears quickly enough, in the person of the Shepherd. Preferring to let the secret remain buried, the Shepherd tries to avoid answering the questions Oedipus asks him. That tactic elicits threats of torture and death from Oedipus, who is bound and determined to know what the Shepherd so desperately wishes not to tell.

The secret is revealed very quickly once the Shepherd decides that there's no point in trying to squash the truth any longer. The baby that Jocasta and Laius abandoned was the same baby who was raised at Corinth and who came home to Thebes to kill Laius and marry the dead king's bride.

Oedipus quickly realizes the horror of what he has been told, and he rushes offstage to nurse his sorrow.

The Chorus reacts by first singing of the glorious achievements Oedipus won for himself in the world. An ancient Athenian

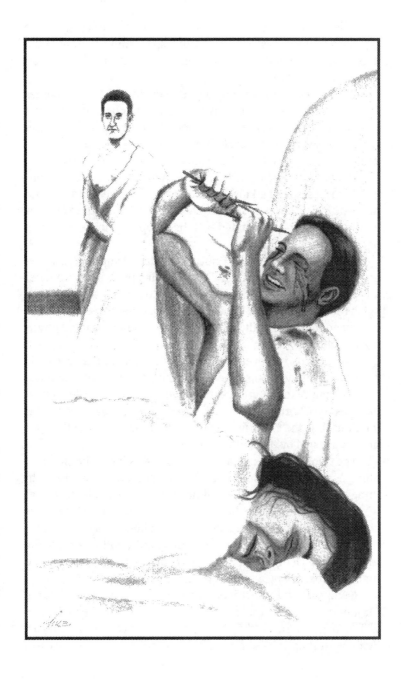

example of the best and brightest of men, he was mighty, he was clever and he was just. But that didn't spare him from being the most awfully cursed individual that anyone in the Chorus can imagine, the members say.

Piling tragedy atop tragedy, a Messenger from the palace comes onstage to announce that Jocasta has taken her own life. He gives the Chorus every ghastly detail—how she tore her hair from her head on her way to the royal bedroom, how she bolted the doors shut behind her and how she wailed with grief and sorrow.

Oedipus is also beside himself with misery, and the Messenger describes how the king followed Jocasta to the bedroom and broke down the doors. Inside the chamber, Oedipus discovered his wife and mother—suspended with her head in a noose, swinging back and forth, dead.

The Messenger tells the Chorus that after Oedipus gently lowered Jocasta's body and laid it down, the king pulled pins from her and blinded himself, driving the points of the long shafts again and again into his eyes. As he blinds himself, Oedipus rages that he has long been metaphorically blind and now he chooses to be physically blind.

The Chorus is moved to pity, but shudders at the gruesome sight of the blinded king, blood streaming down his face, publicly pleading guilty to the crimes that have just been revealed. Oedipus tells the Chorus that he has chosen blindness because maiming himself is the one thing he has ever done in his life that was not prophesied by the gods.

The Chorus answers that it is better to die than to be alive and blind, but Oedipus insists that his self-mutilation was the right thing to do. At least now he will not have to see his father's eyes when they meet in death, he says. He also can't bear to look at his children, his kinsmen or the people of Thebes, he says.

Creon comes onstage, flanked by guards, and he orders the men to bring Oedipus deep inside the palace to spare the ruined man from becoming a public spectacle.

Oedipus begs Creon for banishment, requests a decent burial for Jocasta, and asks that his daughters be looked after. His sons will manage, he says—they are men and they can always make a living with their hands if need be. But the girls were princesses

reared for marriage to royal men, and they have no hope of finding husbands now, Oedipus says.

Creon grants all these requests, and brings the girls to Oedipus for farewell embraces. Oedipus apologizes to them for the
horrors they must now live with and begs them to somehow find a
way to transcend the awful circumstances of their lives.

The play ends with the Chorus saying that, despite his might
and brilliance, Oedipus has ended up crushed by sorrow. If this
can happen to Oedipus, the man who solved the riddle of the
Sphinx and who became a mighty king, it can happen to anyone,
the Chorus says.

Analysis

It took years for fate to catch up with Oedipus and Jocasta, but
once it did it moved very, very quickly. From the beginning of this
section through the last lines of the play, the storyline's momentum accelerates until it becomes unstoppable. The discovery of one
fact leads to the revelation of another, and they accumulate quickly
into destruction. The audience watches the culmination of everything that has come before, knowing that all that was foretold is
now coming to pass.

Jocasta is the first to guess the truth, and it is so unbearable
that she rushes to her chamber and takes her own life. It is possible that Oedipus could have saved her, but her anguish, which is
so palpable to everyone else, is obscured for him by the urgency of
his desire to learn what he still does not know.

His quest is rewarded soon enough. His reaction mixes grief
and shame with wounded pride, and he puts out his own eyes. This
self-mutilation is a mad act of defiance, because it is the one fact
of his life that no god has prophesied.

Creon takes the throne in an unchallenged coup, ending up
through no action of his own exactly where Oedipus accused him
of plotting to be.

Oedipus entrusts his two daughters to Creon's care, saying that
with their marriage prospects totally blighted and the career world
a men-only place they must be protected. The new ruler promises
the broken, blind king that he will take care of the two little girls,
Antigone and Ismene. Oedipus says he is less worried about his

sons. They will be more able than his daughters to make places in the world for themselves because men have more opportunities, he says.

The play ends with the Chorus drawing a pragmatic lesson from the story the members have just witnessed. If the mighty king Oedipus can end up as the plaything of fate, cursed by the gods and crushed by sorrow, then no human beings are safe from tragedy so long as they draw breath.

Study Questions

1. Why does Jocasta say that Oedipus is doomed and run from his sight?

2. When the queen runs off in obvious anguish, why does the Leader of the Chorus seem to have more empathy than Oedipus does?

3. Why is the Shepherd reluctant to answer the questions that Oedipus asks?

4. How does Oedipus react when the Shepherd reveals the truth?

5. How does the Chorus react to the truth the Shepherd reveals?

6. How does the Messenger from the palace preface his news when he announces that Jocasta has taken her own life?

7. How does the audience learn the details of Jocasta's suicide?

8. Who takes down Jocasta's body from the noose ?

9. Why does Oedipus blind himself?

10. How do the final pieces of the story fall into place?

Answers

1. Jocasta says that Oedipus is doomed and she runs from his sight because she has figured out the truth. He still doesn't see how fate has shaped their lives.

2. The Leader of the Chorus seems to have more empathy than Oedipus does because he is not focused only on his own desires, as Oedipus is.

3. The Shepherd is reluctant to answer the questions that Oedipus asks because he is afraid that he will be killed if he speaks the awful truth.

4. When the Shepherd finally reveals the truth, Oedipus shouts that the light will soon go from him now that the deeds of his cursed life have been revealed.

5. The Chorus reacts to the truth the Shepherd reveals with pity, sorrow, and disgust. First recounting the king's great achievements and then listing his crimes, the Chorus ends this speech with sorrowful weeping.

6. When the Messenger from the palace announces that Jocasta has taken her own life, he prefaces the news by asking pity for the royal family and by saying that the palace will never be washed clean of what has happened there.

7. The audience learns the details of Jocasta's suicide when the Messenger tells his tale to the Chorus.

8. Oedipus takes down Jocasta's body from the noose with which she has hung herself.

9. Oedipus blinds himself because he cannot bear to see the faces of his parents when he dies and joins the kingdom of the dead, because he cannot bear to look at his children or the people of Thebes, and because self-mutilation is the one fact of his life that the gods did not predict. It is a mad statement of free will in the face of fate.

10. The final pieces of the story fall into place with an inevitability caused by the prophesies of the gods and the actions of human beings who try to resist fate.

Suggested Essay Topics

1. It takes a great effort by Oedipus to discover the truth about his life. He had to ask the Messenger from Corinth a lot of questions, and he had to send for the old Shepherd. Before the Shepherd even arrives, Jocasta figures out the truth, and promptly takes her own life. Could a less curious and less driven man have avoided the chain of events that led to the

fatal revelations? If Oedipus had been less curious and less driven, would the prophecy have worked itself out another way?

2. The Chorus changes its attitude toward Oedipus and Jocasta more than once. Discuss these attitude changes and how they mesh or conflict with what seems to be genuine sorrow expressed by the Chorus over the fall of the royal family at the end of the play.

3. The King and Queen of Corinth, Polybus and Merope, raised Oedipus as their natural son and never told him he was a foundling, saved from death by starvation on a barren hillside. How much responsibility do they bear for the tragedies of their adopted son's life?

Oedipus at Colonus

Lines 1 – 524

New Characters:

Oedipus: *the former King of Thebes*

Antigone: *the daughter of Oedipus and Jocasta*

A Citizen: *a citizen or free man of Colonus*

Chorus: *a group of elders from Colonus and their Leader, whose commentary helps the audience understand the events on stage*

Ismene: *the daughter of Oedipus and Jocasta*

Summary

The play begins with Oedipus, who was once a mighty king, as a broken, blind, exiled wanderer. Antigone, a young woman who is both his daughter and his sister, serves Oedipus as his eyes, his guide and his only companion.

After long years of wandering and begging, Oedipus has learned humility. He is grateful now for any small kindness he is shown. He has also learned acceptance. Although he mourns the tragedies of his life—killing his father, marrying his mother and fathering children who are his siblings—the rage he once felt toward the gods is gone.

At the beginning of the play, Oedipus and Antigone stumble upon a grove that looks like a nice place for a rest. As these two tragic figures are making themselves comfortable, a citizen of the

city appears. He announces that the strangers have trespassed on a sacred grove. The man is angry with the trespassers, and he fears divine retribution.

Oedipus wants to know to whom the grove is sacred, and when the Citizen says that it is dedicated to the Eumenides—known also as the Furies—a mystical joy seizes the blind, exiled king.

Thoroughly rattled now, the citizen turns to leave. He is confused by this encounter—angry over the trespassing, fearful of the wrath of the goddesses and baffled by the behavior of this ragged pair of beggars—and he wants to get someone else's opinion about it all.

Oedipus detains him, and questions the man about the city and its ruler. Recognizing that Oedipus is some sort of aristocrat in dire straits, the citizen stays for a few moments, but his fear soon proves to be his strongest emotion. The citizen then leaves to find stronger, wiser people to deal with this situation.

With the citizen gone, Oedipus asks Antigone to make sure they are alone. Once she says that there's no one in sight, Oedipus prays fervently to the Eumenides. Oedipus tells the goddesses that he has reached the final chapter of his life, and he asks them to balance all his tragedies with their blessings. He knows that the prophecy that shaped his life has a final, unfinished part—that he will render a great gift to the people who shelter him at the end of his life. He says he is ready for that to happen now. As he finishes his prayer, Antigone sees people coming. She urges Oedipus to hide, and they take cover in the sacred grove.

The news travels fast, and the Chorus comes onstage as an angry mob bent on punishing the wandering beggar who has trampled on sacred ground. The mob demands to know who has committed this crime. Stepping forward with Antigone's help, Oedipus presents himself to the Chorus. The mob's mood changes to pity for the blind old man. The Chorus begs him to step out of the grove before he angers the goddesses more by profaning their shrine.

Oedipus says he will leave the sacred ground only if the mob promises him safety. The Chorus makes the deal, and Antigone leads Oedipus forward, step by step. Taking a seat on the rocks beyond the sacred grove's boundary, Oedipus is questioned by the Chorus. At first, he attempts to evade their questions about his

identity with pleas for privacy, but Oedipus soon answers with a question of his own.

Asking if the Chorus knows a man who is the son of Laius, the one time King of Thebes, Oedipus hands the men the keys to his history.

The Chorus reacts quickly and brutally, telling him that he must leave immediately and go far, far away. Worse, the Chorus says that the promise of protection given to Oedipus is now invalid, because it was granted before he revealed who he is.

Antigone begs for mercy for her father and for herself, saying that every human being on earth must fulfill whatever prophecy the gods lay down. Oedipus could not escape doing what the gods foretold, and the Chorus should pity him, not chastise him.

The Leader of the Chorus says he feels sorry for the young woman and her shattered father, but he fears what the gods may do if the unhappy pair is allowed to stay. Oedipus answers the Leader's fear with a mighty speech that shows some flashes of the wit and courage that were his when he wore the crown of Thebes. Oedipus argues that the crimes he committed as a young man— killing his father and marrying his mother—were the acts of an innocent man who was unwittingly fulfilling the prophecy of the gods.

He ends this speech by saying that just as the gods steered him to blindly and unknowingly commit acts that he spent his life trying to avoid, so the Chorus must now do what the gods wish by sheltering him. Oedipus announces that he is someone sacred now, someone filled with piety and power, who will soon bestow a great gift. He asks to be treated fairly in the meantime.

Speaking for the Chorus, the Leader says that Oedipus is an awesome man, but nothing can be settled until Theseus, the King of Athens, arrives. A messenger has already been sent, and Theseus is sure to come when he hears who the wanderer is, the Leader says.

Just then, Antigone sees her sister, Ismene, riding toward them on a swift colt. Ismene comes bringing news that is so important she cannot trust it to a messenger, she says. Oedipus asks why her brothers, Polynices and Eteocles, couldn't have spared her the trip and come themselves. Ismene says that her brothers couldn't come because they now face their darkest hour.

Oedipus is too angry at his sons to be worried about what Ismene says, and he berates them for leaving their filial burdens to their sisters. During all the long years of exile, Antigone has wandered with him and Ismene has brought news of oracles and kings, but his sons have done nothing, Oedipus says.

Ismene reveals the fresh news from the oracles and from the palace, and it is profound. Back in Thebes, the people who sent Oedipus into exile now want him back. The gods have decided to use Oedipus for a great purpose, Ismene says, and Creon, the current leader of Thebes, wants that great purpose fulfilled within his sight.

Thebes has been warned that it will be cursed if Oedipus is buried without the proper funeral rites, Ismene says. The leaders want to bring him back to make sure that happens, but there's a catch. They will not bury him inside the city because of his past, Ismene says.

This infuriates Oedipus, who says that he will never allow the Thebans to seize him now. If they won't give him a burial inside the city, let them be cursed. Ismene reveals that his reaction was more or less predicted by the prophecy, which goes on to say that the enemies of Oedipus will one day trod the ground where he is buried and they will be destroyed by his rage.

Oedipus asks Ismene whether her two brothers have heard these latest updates from the oracles. She says they have, and they have ignored the news. Enraged by their lack of interest, Oedipus calls down a fearsome curse on his sons. He asks the gods to prevent any outbreak of peace between the two warring young men. They didn't help him when he was sentenced to exile, and they haven't done anything for him in all the long years since then, he says.

Oedipus turns from cursing his sons to thanking the gods for his daughters. Then he tells the Chorus that if he is defended now he will deliver this land from danger later. He will also wreak destruction on his human enemies. The Leader of the Chorus is filled with pity and awe, and he agrees to help.

Analysis

Oedipus at Colonus is a wanderer's tale. It picks up the story told in *Oedipus the King* some years later. Jocasta, the Queen of

Thebes, is long dead. Oedipus, her husband, blinded himself years ago and has been an exiled beggar for some time.

Years of wandering and begging have made Oedipus almost unrecognizable. No longer the proud king he was in his youth, he has learned to be grateful for the small rations that beggars receive. He has also put away his rage against the gods.

When he was young, Oedipus mocked the gods, and thought himself clever for outrunning the destiny they foretold. When he learned that his every action had led him closer, faster, to what he was avoiding, he bowed for the first time to divine power.

He has since respected that power, and he is awed and glad when he stumbles into the grove that is sacred to the Eumenides, who are known in one of their manifestations as the Kindly Ones.

The Eumenides were part of the cultural inheritance of the ancient world, and even people who no longer believed in the old religion knew the stories about them. Appearing in human affairs sometimes as the Kindly Ones and sometimes as the Furies, they took particular interest in how people satisfied or failed to meet the obligations of kinship.

In the ancient world, the gods were highly specialized, and they also took things that human beings did personally. They meted out rewards and punishments accordingly. Occasionally, whole cities and kingdoms benefitted or were cursed by individual gods. That tradition carried over into Christianity in the form of patron saints.

The Eumenides took as one of their responsibilities the protection of Athens, and that means a great deal to Oedipus. Once he arrives at their sacred grove, he desires only to die and be buried in the realm where they rule.

For the first time since his life unraveled, Oedipus now sees a chance to balance the many tragedies he has both caused and endured. Clinging to remembered shreds of the prophecy that shaped his life, Oedipus remembers that there is one part yet to be fulfilled. It was foretold that he will be able to offer a great gift to his benefactors at the end of his days. He interprets this to mean that if he is allowed to die here, the Athenian people will collect a magnificent reward.

The remembered prophecy is one shred of the person Oedipus once was, but there are others; the glories and griefs of his other

memories. Tattered, destitute, and blind though he is, Oedipus is still the man who solved the riddle of the Sphinx, freeing Thebes from the Sphinx's bloodthirsty appetites. That triumph led, unfortunately, to the Thebans awarding him as his wife their widowed queen, Jocasta.

Oedipus reveals a little of his old cleverness when he extracts a promise of protection from the Chorus before he reveals his identity. The riddle before him this time is how to win shelter and protection from them when he is a pariah whose very name evokes disgust. He solves it by appealing for mercy when his name is still known only to him and Antigone.

The one time king goes on to display a little of the power he once commanded over people. When the Chorus discovers who he is and wants to send him away, his arguments make it clear that he still retains the ability to bend people to his will, although his only crown now is one of pain.

Demanding shelter and mercy in a long and moving speech to the Chorus, Oedipus strikes several themes. One theme of this profoundly emotional speech is that the renown Oedipus enjoyed as a king is worthless to him if it means nothing to these people now. Glory and fame are fleeting, and they last only as long as people's memories of them do.

Another theme that Oedipus works with is the idea that the proud citizens of this kingdom can hardly continue to honor themselves for the virtues they show if they fail to shelter him. Charity and generosity are qualities that are nice to talk about, but the Chorus is about to miss an opportunity to act on them, Oedipus says.

Finally, Oedipus goes on to mock the Chorus for being afraid to shelter him, saying that he is too weak to hurt anyone.

Later in this section, the news from Ismene fills Oedipus with joy. The Oracle's words have—at last—the power to balance the agonies of his life. He is so cheered that he cracks a rueful little joke, saying it is easy for the gods to raise up someone they have already crushed.

When he explains Ismene's news to the Chorus, saying that he can one day destroy the enemies of those who shelter him, along with his own foes, Oedipus states these new facts as boldly as if they had always been true. Another flash of his former greatness and power illuminates the scene.

Study Questions

1. What has Oedipus learned from his years of begging and wandering in exile?

2. Where do Oedipus and Antigone tread at the beginning of the play?

3. How does the Citizen react to the strangers in the sacred grove?

4. What prayer does Oedipus offer after the Citizen leaves?

5. How does the Chorus react at first to the news that someone has trespassed on the sacred grove?

6. How does the Chorus react when Oedipus, haggard and blind, reveals himself?

7. How does the Chorus react when Oedipus gives his name?

8. How does Oedipus shame the Chorus into accepting him?

9. What news does Ismene bring?

10. How does Oedipus react to Ismene's news?

Answers

1. From his years of begging and wandering in exile, Oedipus has learned humility and he has learned acceptance.

2. At the beginning of the play, Oedipus and Antigone tread on a grove that is sacred to the Eumenides.

3. The Citizen reacts to the strangers in the sacred grove with a mixture of anger and fear. He is angry that they have trespassed, and he is fearful of divine retribution.

4. After the Citizen leaves, Oedipus prays to the Eumenides in both their manifestations—kindly and punishing—and he asks them to give him the great gift promised by the gods that will balance the agonies of his younger years.

5. The Chorus reacts like an angry mob to the news that someone has trespassed on the sacred grove.

6. The Chorus reacts with pity when Oedipus, haggard and blind, reveals himself.

7. The Chorus reacts with fear and disgust when Oedipus tells them his name.

8. Oedipus shames the Chorus into accepting him in several ways. He appeals to the Athenian tradition of compassion and charity toward strangers, and he claims that the terrible crimes he unknowingly committed were the acts of an innocent man who was the plaything of the gods. He also says that the gods are watching right now to see how the Chorus treats him.

9. Ismene brings news that Creon, her uncle, is trying to get Oedipus back to Thebes because the city will be cursed unless Oedipus is buried properly. But that plan does not include burial inside the gates of Thebes, which infuriates Oedipus.

10. Oedipus reacts to Ismene's news with joy and vindication, saying that he knew the gods had something great set aside for him after all his suffering.

Suggested Essay Topics

1. By reacting to Oedipus in several different ways in this first section of the play, the Chorus reveals some ageless truths about human nature. So does the Citizen who first discovers the strangers in the sacred grove. Discuss how fear, indecision, awe and pity mix in these characters' reactions, and discuss how they act on their feelings.

2. Ismene brings amazing news. Oedipus, in death, will have the power to crush the foes of his final protectors along with his own enemies. It seems as if the gods have finally decided to do something good for him after fashioning an earlier destiny of unremitting pain. What kind of a bargain is it really? Is the power of revenge an even exchange for a life wrecked by grief? Is revenge worth that much? Discuss.

3. What emotional changes does Oedipus undergo in this section. Why?

Lines 525 – 1,192

New Characters:

Theseus: *the King of Athens, which includes Colonus*

Creon: *the King of Thebes, and the brother of Jocasta*

Summary

Now that the Leader has gathered his courage and agreed to help Oedipus, the next step is to make amends to the goddesses whose ground was trespassed upon. This section begins with Oedipus and the Leader acting as tutor and teacher in a complex religious ritual meant to soothe the Eumenides into forgiveness. The complicated ritual involves sacred water, tufts of wool cut from a young lamb and olive branches. Olives were one of the crops that Greek traders sold on their land-and-sea routes, and it was also a basic element of the people's daily diet. The Leader tells Oedipus the words of the simple but profound prayer that is part of the ritual. It is a plea for mercy from the goddesses, who are recognized as mighty but kind.

Oedipus listens carefully to all this, and then says that he is too old and frail to perform the work. He asks his daughters to help him by gathering the offerings for the ceremony, and they both offer to do the work. Ismene says that Antigone should stay by their father's side, where she has served so faithfully for so long. They agree, and Ismene leaves to collect the things the goddesses require.

Immediately, the Chorus closes around Oedipus. The old men insist on being told every awful detail of his life. He begs them to stop prying, and he makes a small plea for help to the gods, but the Chorus keeps probing.

Convinced that the Chorus will not be quiet until he satisfies the raging curiosity now focused on him, Oedipus tells his sad tale. As he details the crimes he committed—killing his father, marrying his mother and fathering children who are both his offspring and his siblings—the Chorus urges Oedipus on with little sighs and whispers of empathy. Throughout the telling, Oedipus owns up to his deeds, but he insists on his fundamental innocence. By his reasoning, the fact that the true nature of his actions was hidden from him at the time he committed them makes him an innocent man.

He does not shrink from the horror of his deeds in the telling, nor does he deny that he committed them. But he insists that a man whose fate was foretold before he was born cannot really be blamed for fulfilling the prophecy laid down by the gods.

This dialogue is interrupted by the arrival of Theseus, the King of Athens. He has come as summoned, which was predicted in the first section of the play.

The opening speech of the Athenian king reveals a man who blends compassion and justice with courage and wisdom. His first response to the tattered, blind, old beggar is to offer aid and comfort. He ends his remarks by saying that he cannot foretell the future—he can only act decently and generously in the present.

Oedipus reacts with joy to the unconditional offer of aid, and promises Theseus a great gift in return. The king asks what the gift is and when it will be available. Oedipus says that Theseus will know what the gift is soon enough, but its effects won't be felt until the wandering beggar is cold in his grave.

Explaining the terms of the gift, Oedipus says that it will save Athens from an invading Theban army. This makes no sense at all to Theseus, who says that Athens and Thebes enjoy cordial relations. Oedipus says that those relations are as changeable as the wind. Everything that human beings know and love will wither and die in time, Oedipus says, and everything they see today will be gone tomorrow. Only the gods endure forever.

Oedipus closes this meditation on mortality and eternity by saying that spears will be thrown at each other one day by the people of Thebes and Athens. If he is allowed to have his wish and if he is buried in Athenian ground, then the Theban soldiers will die when they cross his tomb, Oedipus says.

Theseus proves himself wise and just once again, saying that even without such a gift he owes Oedipus shelter. He offers the wanderer the full rights and privileges of Athenian citizenship. As he prepares to leave, Theseus reiterates his assurances.

The Chorus then delivers a long, lyrical paean to Colonus in particular and Athens in general, praising its earthly and divine attributes. Its birds, vines and olive groves are praised, and its patron goddess, Athena, is honored. Credit is given to Athenian horsemanship and Athenian sailing ships—two forces that brought the kingdom greatness.

The last echoes of this song have not yet faded when Antigone announces that she sees Creon coming, accompanied by an escort. Oedipus begs the Chorus to remember the pledge of protection Theseus gave, and asks the men to defend him to the end. The Leader of the Chorus answers that his country is still strong, although he is weak, and Oedipus will be defended.

Creon arrives, and he soothes and flatters the Chorus into letting him speak to Oedipus. In an instant, the current King of Thebes launches a barrage of insults and threats at Oedipus, the blind and broken former king. Calling his former brother-in-law a stumbling beggar who should be ashamed to be seen on the public roads, Creon wraps his insults in pity and says he feels sorry for Oedipus. More insults glide from Creon's mouth, and he says that Antigone has been degraded by her long years of wandering with her wrecked father. Creon ends this attempt at persuasion and intimidation by all but ordering Oedipus to come back with him to Thebes.

Oedipus may be a blind, frail, old beggar, but he is still the man who was renowned near and far as a great king, and Creon's words inspire no fear in him, moving him only to rage. He says that Creon never helped him years ago when he needed it, making it highly unlikely that any help offered now is truly what it seems. Then he openly calls Creon a liar, saying that he knows that the current king intends to carry him back to Thebes but bury him just outside the city's gates.

Creon answers with gentle solicitousness, saying that Oedipus hurts himself more than anyone else with such harsh words. When that suggestion is laughed away by Oedipus, the truth comes out and Creon reverts to insult-hurling.

Oedipus tells Creon to go away and leave him alone, and then Creon plays his trump card. On his way to the grove, his party met and seized Ismene, he says. He intends now to seize Antigone, too.

Oedipus and the Leader of the Chorus join in condemning Creon for these actions, and Creon threatens war if any of the Athenian men touch him. Creon's guards drag Antigone away, and he tells Oedipus that she and Ismene will never see their father again.

Creon turns to leave, but the Chorus blocks his way. He threatens to seize Oedipus, too, who curses him in old age. Just as Creon takes hold of Oedipus, Theseus appears and comes to the rescue.

Theseus heard the noise and the struggle from far off, and he came running back, he says. Oedipus tells him that Ismene and Antigone have been kidnapped by Creon's thugs, and Theseus orders a full-scale search. Turning angrily to Creon, Theseus tells him that his crimes against the women and their father will not go unpunished.

Theseus decides that Creon will be held captive in Athens until the sisters are returned. He tells Creon that Athens is a place of justice and courage, and that brutality will not be tolerated. Kidnapping the women from Athenian soil is a major act of disrespect, and it will not pass unnoticed, Theseus says. Creon responds by saying that he acted as he did because he never expected anyone as righteous as the Athenians to offer shelter to anyone as criminal as Oedipus.

Stepping into the argument and answering with proud fury, Oedipus says that Creon is the criminal. Every heinous act that Oedipus committed, and he admits to them all, looked perfectly reasonable on the surface. It was his grim fate that the real meaning of his actions only became apparent to him years later, he says. Again, as when he told his life story to the Chorus, Oedipus maintains his basic innocence.

But the things that Creon is doing are evil, Oedipus says. Kidnapping, holding up for public scrutiny yet again the sad story of his sister Jocasta's incestuous marriage to Oedipus—these deeds are bad and they are wrong, by any standard, any place, any time, Oedipus says.

This long speech closes with a prayer to the Eumenides. Oedipus asks them to teach Creon a lesson.

The Leader of the Chorus then confirms everything that Oedipus has said, and tells Theseus that Oedipus deserves help. Seizing the moment, Theseus says that the time for talking is over. Kidnappers are riding off with Ismene and Antigone, and this is no time to be standing around and arguing.

Theseus orders Creon to lead a search party for the guards and the young women. He tells Creon that he and his co-conspirators, whoever they are, will find no mercy from anyone. Creon proves again that he is an unfit king, and he makes bold noises about the help waiting for him back in Thebes

This section ends with Theseus vowing never to stop searching for Ismene and Antigone until he finds them, and Oedipus expressing his deep gratitude.

Analysis

The audiences who first watched the play knew all the background in advance, because the life stories of these characters were part of the cultural fabric of ancient Greece. But the spectacle of Oedipus reviewing all the tawdry details of his life in answer to prying and prurient questions from the Chorus was sad and compelling theater then, as it is now.

Thus, the tragic history of the House of Oedipus is told as part of the action of the play, through the dramatic device of a question-and-answer session between Oedipus and the Chorus. We hear how Oedipus discovered that the stranger he had killed on a highway was his natural father, Laius, the King of Thebes. He tells how he married the widowed queen without knowing that she was his natural mother, Jocasta. We hear how Antigone and Ismene, the daughters of the ill-fated marriage of Oedipus and Jocasta, came to be both their father's children and his sisters, just as Polynices and Eteocles, the sons of that marriage, are both their father's sons and brothers.

Throughout this recitation, Oedipus maintains that he committed all his crimes unwittingly, as the plaything of the gods, who kept the true meaning of his deeds secret from him until long after they were done. This makes him an innocent man, he says, because he did only what the gods foretold.

Later, in his confrontation with Creon, Oedipus makes the argument again, and more strongly this time. If the prophecy that would shape his life was delivered before his birth, as it was, how can he be blamed for fulfilling a divine mandate?

It is an interesting argument, because it combines the moral and intellectual questions that flow most deeply through all three of these plays. When human beings act, how freely do they make their decisions? Is everything already planned by the gods? Do people only think they are controlling their own destinies? Is fate such a pre-determined thing that there is no escape?

In these confrontations between Oedipus and the Chorus and Oedipus and Creon, much of the dramatic action is psychological. We see the Chorus wheedling information from Oedipus, and we see him deciding that it is best to deal with their prurient curiosity by satisfying it with the details of his life. He is covered with shame and bowed with grief when he begins his story, but he gathers strength as he maintains his innocence.

Later, when Oedipus is verbally dueling with Creon, the manipulativeness of both men is on full display. They exchange barbs for some minutes before Creon reveals that Ismene has been seized. Oedipus reacts to the kidnapping of his daughters by allowing his anger full reign. He allows himself the privilege of hurling insults at Creon, a reigning king, that he can only get away with if his new Athenian brothers support him as they pledged they would.

Theseus appears at a crucial moment, keeping his word, and thoroughly humiliates Creon, saying that the Theban King will be a prisoner in Athens until the women are returned. It turns out that Oedipus calculated correctly when he put his faith in Theseus, who helps a frail, blind beggar triumph over the scheming Creon.

The dramatic tension has built to a high peak in this section, and many possibilities are now coiled like springs.

Ismene and Antigone are in serious danger. Oedipus and Creon—the fallen ruler and the current king—have feuded publicly, and grave consequences are likely. Most serious of all, Theseus, the King of Athens, has taken Creon's assaults on Ismene, Antigone and Oedipus as insults to the Athenian people and to his own throne, raising the possibility of war.

Study Questions

1. What ceremony does the Leader of the Chorus explain to Oedipus?

2. How does Oedipus react when the Leader finishes explaining the ceremony?

3. What do Ismene and Antigone say after their father speaks to the Leader about the ceremony?

4. Why does the Chorus want Oedipus to recite the details of his life?

5. Why does Oedipus yield to the curiosity of the Chorus when the men press him for the details of his life?

6. Why does Theseus offer protection and the full rights of citizenship to Oedipus?

7. What gift does Oedipus promise to Theseus?

8. Why is Creon searching for Oedipus?

9. Why does Creon seize Ismene and Antigone?

10. Why will Creon be Theseus' prisoner until the women are returned?

Answers

1. The Leader of the Chorus explains to Oedipus how to make an offering to the Eumenides, the goddesses whose sacred grove has been trod upon.

2. When the Leader finishes explaining the ceremony, Oedipus says that he is too old and weak to perform the rituals. He asks Ismene and Antigone if one of them could take his place.

3. Ismene says that she will gather what the goddesses require and she will perform the rites. She tells Antigone to stay and watch over their father, and Antigone makes no protest.

4. The Chorus wants Oedipus to recite the details of his life for the prurient thrill of hearing the story, which everyone already knows, from the lips of the man who was one of its main characters.

5. Oedipus wants to tell them that he believes he is fundamentally innocent, because the true nature of his crimes was hidden from him.

6. Theseus offer protection and the full rights of citizenship to Oedipus because Athens prides itself on being a kingdom where compassion and justice are honored, because he has pity for a blind, old man who was once a mighty king and

because it is right and proper to offer charity to people need-
ing help.

7. Oedipus promises Theseus that if he is allowed to die and
    be buried in Athens, his tomb will destroy any of the
    kingdom's enemies who trod on it, forever.

8. Creon wants to talk his former brother-in-law, Oedipus, into
    coming back to Thebes so that he cannot become a deadly
    trap for Theban soldiers.

9. Creon seizes Ismene and Antigone because he believes that
    kidnapping the women will intimidate Oedipus into com-
    ing back to Thebes.

10. Theseus vows that Creon will be his prisoner until the
    women are returned because the kidnapping was a crime
    and because Theseus takes it personally as an insult to him
    and to his kingdom.

Suggested Essay Topics

1. Theseus is portrayed as a kind, just and generous king who
    defends the honor of his kingdom when he tells Creon that
    assaults against Ismene, Antigone and Oedipus will not be
    tolerated. Why does Theseus do this? What traditions and
    philosophies is Theseus upholding?

2. Creon wants Oedipus to be buried properly, in order to pre-
    vent Thebes from bearing a curse, but he wants the grave to
    be outside the gates of the city. When he attempts to talk
    Oedipus into this plan, he is prepared to use force. He thinks
    he can get away with making threats against young women
    and an old man without interference from Theseus. Discuss
    what makes Creon act the way he does.

3. Oedipus is prepared to die, but first he wants everyone to
    know that he believes his crimes to have been destined, and
    beyond his control. How does fate shape human lives? Can
    we escape fate's grasp? Oedipus thought he could, and he
    wound up running toward his destiny. Discuss.

Lines 1,193 – 1,645

New Character:

Polynices: *the son of Oedipus and Jocasta*

Summary

Imagining glorious victory for the Athenians and crushing defeat for the enemy, the Chorus describes images of war. The battle-lust ends suddenly, when the Leader tells Oedipus that Ismene and Antigone are in sight.

The two women appear, accompanied by Theseus, their rescuer, and they rush into their father's embrace. Oedipus thanks Theseus, and praises him in general and Athens in particular for showing a blind, broken old man the first truth and justice he has seen in all his wanderings. Theseus modestly accepts the praise, and reaffirms his promises of protection. He declines to boast of the battle that won the women back, saying that such talk is not his style. Going on to prove himself not only brave, but honest, truthful and just, Theseus shows that he is meticulous, too, when he tells Oedipus that someone is looking for the wanderer. Theseus met the man at the altar for sacrifices to Poseidon, where each made an offering.

Theseus tells Oedipus that the man just wants a word with the wanderer, to whom he claims kinship. But when Theseus says that the man is from Argos, Oedipus tells him to stop. Theseus presses the point, and Oedipus says that the man must be Polynices. This son has caused Oedipus more pain than anyone else on earth.

Theseus says that may be so, but what could it hurt to listen to someone who has traveled a long way for a visit? Theseus suggests that Oedipus should see the visitor, if for no other reason that it might please the gods.

Antigone joins in, saying that Oedipus owes it to Theseus, the gods, and to her, her sister and himself to see Polynices. She tells Oedipus that he isn't the only father in the world who has been furious with an unfaithful son, and if others are capable of forgiveness then he should be, too. She ends her plea by reminding Oedipus of the suffering he and his parents endured in their relationships and says that he has a chance to break this cycle of pain now.

Not because he wants to, but because he cannot deny Antigone a plea that she so clearly believes in, Oedipus agrees to see Polynices. He asks Theseus to stand by in case of trouble, and Theseus again vows that so long as the gods protect him he will protect Oedipus.

The Chorus comments on all that has come before with a long, mournful speech that describes human life as suffering and pain and says that the only way to be free of misery is to never be born. All happiness ends in sorrow, and youth yields to lonely old age, the Chorus says.

As the echoes of these words fade, Antigone announces that she sees Polynices coming. The visitor arrives, and he sounds sincere when he says that he pities Oedipus and the women. Polynices calls himself the worst man on earth, but he adds that as the gods can be merciful, so Oedipus should be willing to let go of old hurts. He expands his plea to the women, calling on them to use their influence with their father in his behalf. Antigone seems willing to give Polynices the benefit of the doubt, and tells her brother to continue his tale and to explain why he has sought them out now.

Polynices begins his story, saying first that he is under the protection of Theseus, just as they are, an assertion that shows he is a coward who is afraid of a broken old man and two women. He continues, reciting the tale of how he demanded the right to sit on the Theban throne in the days after Oedipus was disgraced. For that, his brother, Eteocles, gathered the political will and power to drive Polynices out of the country. He has lived now many years in exile, like his father, he says. Polynices settled in Argos, where he married. He now intends to launch a war against Thebes to regain the throne he still thinks is rightfully his. Creon, his uncle, sits on that throne now, supported by Eteocles. Polynices ends this tale by asking Oedipus to guarantee his victory by joining his side.

Oedipus reacts with the full fury of a man who has been nursing a grudge for a long time and now finally has the chance to do something about it. Rejecting both his son's pity and his plea, Oedipus calls down a mighty curse on Polynices—the same one he placed on Polynices years ago. Oedipus reminds Polynices that if the gods have any sense of justice left, the curse will be fulfilled, and Polynices and Eteocles will murder each other in this coming war. Filling the air with threats, curses and prayers, Oedipus vents his wrath on Polynices until the Leader of the Chorus suggests that it is time for the visitor to leave.

Polynices utters a few self-pitying words about the doom that awaits him, and begs his sisters to give him a decent burial at the end of it all. Antigone answers with a plea of her own, saying that Polynices could save everyone a lot of trouble by calling off this war and turning back his army. But his pride and his thirst for power overcome every other feeling or thought he has, and Polynices insists that the battle must go forward.

It is clear to Antigone that her brother is about to fulfill their father's curse, and that he and Eteocles will commit mutual murder if this battle proceeds as scheduled. She begs Polynices again to stop, saying that no soldiers will fight for him once they hear the prophecy that says he cannot win, and he says he'll deal with that by keeping the prophecy a secret.

This section ends with Polynices vowing to fight, and as he leaves Antigone begins to mourn him as if he were already dead.

Analysis

This section begins with the Chorus hysterically excited by the prospect of war. Imagining the clash and clang of a battle between Athens and Thebes, the men predict a mighty victory for the home forces. This blood-lust ends only when the Leader tells Oedipus that Ismene and Antigone are in sight.

This scene reinforces the impressions we have of the Chorus as not necessarily the best and the brightest men that the ancient world had to offer. In the earliest scenes, the men seemed inclined to force Oedipus out of their kingdom when he came in search of aid and comfort. Not until Theseus came along and told them to do the right thing did they show the courage or honor required of just men in a just society.

The idea that these men are sometimes weak and silly is repeated in this scene. Victory in battle was a glorious thing in the ancient world, and the Homeric canon is filled with the soldierly exploits of heroes, but this scene suggests that war is not always a good thing. It is always the young men who fight wars, and it is always the old men who send them to their deaths and cheer them on. The scene ends with prayers to the gods, which are appropriate preparations for war and rumors of war, but a great deal of unseemly battle-lust preceded those prayers.

In the next scene, Theseus escorts Ismene and Antigone into the arms of their father, and the king who rescued them is loath to discuss the details of how he won their freedom. This reticence, plus his quiet determination to do what needs to be done and then get on with things, is in marked contrast to the vainglorious war chants of the Chorus. Theseus suggests by his modesty that battles are sometimes necessary, and they should be fought well and they should be won, but there is a human cost to both sides that is neglected by the glory-seeking old men in the Chorus.

The reunion of Oedipus and his daughters is tender and sweet. As he embraces them, he thanks Theseus for saving them. Theseus reiterates his promises of protection. Theseus goes on to say that someone is looking for Oedipus, and he is startled by the fury Oedipus unleashes after figuring out that the would-be visitor is Polynices.

In the long confrontation between the two men, Oedipus and Polynices prove themselves to be more alike than either would ever admit. Equally fierce, angry and proud, the father and son share the same faults. As the argument escalates and the insults fly, both men continue to embrace destruction like a lover. Hurling curses at his son, Oedipus fails to see that Polynices is as determined to walk into the arms of doom as he was. For his part, Polynices is equally blind to the realization that he is entering the embrace of fate as surely as his disgraced father did.

Once we hear the announcement from Polynices that he intends to pursue his cause and to go forward with a battle that can only result in grief, the largest themes of the play are displayed again.

Do people have any control over their destinies, or is the prophecy of the gods immutable? Can people ever learn from the past or are they doomed to play out the same scenes again and again, through the generations? The answers suggested by the text are not particularly optimistic.

At the end of this section, when Polynices leaves, tragedy is foreshadowed for *Antigone*. That story will not reach its fulfillment in this play, but the outline of *Antigone*, the final play in the lives of these characters, is suggested when Polynices extracts from his sister her promise that she will give him an honorable burial, no matter what. It is easy enough to foresee in that promise that a man who dies as a traitor to the Theban crown could well be denied proper death rituals by a monarch as wild as Creon. It is also easy to imagine that Creon would not take kindly to anyone who violates such a decree.

Study Questions

1. How does Theseus win back Ismene and Antigone?
2. How does Oedipus react when he is reunited with his daughters?
3. What promise does Theseus reaffirm to the family after the reunion?
4. Why does Polynices want to see his father?
5. How does Polynices begin the dialogue with his father?
6. How does Antigone feel about the visit from Polynices?
7. Oedipus reacts to Polynices how?
8. What happens between Oedipus and Polynices as their conversation continues?
9. What curse does Oedipus repeat to Polynices?
10. What promise does Polynices wrest from Antigone?

Answers

1. Theseus wins back Ismene and Antigone by chasing down their captors. He declines to boast of the details.
2. Oedipus reacts with joy and gratitude when he is reunited with his daughters.
3. After the reunion, Theseus reaffirms his promise of protection.
4. Polynices wants to see his father so that the old man's powers will guarantee him victory.

5. Polynices begins the dialogue with his father as a contrite son seeking forgiveness and hoping to set right all the wrongs of the past.

6. When Polynices arrives, Antigone is optimistic and she is willing to forgive her brother. She urges Oedipus to listen to what Polynices wants to say.

7. Oedipus reacts to Polynices with anger and mistrust.

8. As the conversation between Oedipus and Polynices continues, the son reveals his true purpose for coming and the father becomes even more angry.

9. Oedipus repeats to Polynices an old curse, which is that the two brothers will kill each other in battle.

10. Polynices wrests from Antigone the promise of a decent burial, no matter what happens. This does not bode well for Antigone.

Suggested Essay Topics

1. This section opens with a bloodthirsty Chorus lusting for battle. A few scenes later, a victorious Theseus declines to boast of how he won freedom for Antigone and Ismene. At the end of this section, Polynices is ready to fight a war to gain the Theban crown, despite the curses of his father and the advice of Antigone. Compare and contrast the attitudes toward war displayed in this section.

2. Oedipus feels unfathomable rage against Polynices. The old, blind king is as unable to think of negotiating any kind of peace with his power-hungry son as he was able to prevent the fulfillment of the prophecies that shaped his own life. Is there a larger meaning here or is this problem limited to this family at this time in this place? Discuss.

3. Theseus shows yet again in this section how an ideal king behaves. How close to, or far from, this standard are the political leaders you read about in newspapers or hear about on television or on the radio?

Lines 1,646 – 2,001

New Character:

A Messenger: *a messenger who delivers news*

Summary

The rumbling sounds of thunder off in the distance are the sign that Oedipus has been waiting for. He believes that his death is imminent, and he asks that Theseus be brought to him immediately. The Chorus is awestruck by the booming thunder and the sizzling lightning, and the men ask what will happen and where will it end? Calmly and with great certainty, Oedipus turns to his daughters and tells them that his time on earth is expired. As he speaks, the weather redoubles its force. The Chorus trembles, praying for mercy.

The divine force unleashed in the skies frightens even Oedipus, and he fears that Theseus will reach him too late for the message that must be delivered. Oedipus is ready to give Theseus the gift he promised earlier, but the good king must arrive before it is too late.

Eager for the gift to be delivered to their king and to their country, the men in the Chorus urge Theseus on, and he arrives just as they finish speaking. Well aware that lightning bolts flashing across the sky are omens of serious events, Theseus asks what's going on. Oedipus says that this is the moment of his death, and that he is grateful for the opportunity to fulfill the promise he made Theseus. The weather is heralding what must come next, Oedipus says. Theseus asks Oedipus for instructions.

Oedipus says that he will lead the way to the place where he will die and where he is to be buried, and that the location must be a secret even from Ismene and Antigone. So long as the grave remains undisturbed, it will be a powerful shield that will keep the kingdom safe from any enemy, Oedipus says.

Suddenly gathering strength he has not had in years, Oedipus stands up and says good-bye to the earth and the sunlight and to his daughters.

The Chorus offers prayers, asking for justice, peace and eternal sleep for Oedipus in the kingdom of the dead after the many long agonies of his life. As soon as the prayers end, a Messenger enters. His news is that Oedipus is dead, and that the event was witnessed and assisted by the gods. The Leader of the Chorus asks for details, and the Messenger tells what happened.

Leading the way, as if he had suddenly regained sight in his ruined eyes, Oedipus walked to the spot of his choosing and sat down, the Messenger tells the Chorus. Then the old man asked his daughters to bring him water, and he bathed himself and made an offering.

When those ceremonies were complete, Zeus made his thundering presence known. The women shrieked and wailed with fear and grief, the Messenger said. Oedipus soothed them with loving words, and the three embraced and wept.

Then, a divine voice called to Oedipus and told him to hurry, that it was time to be going. Oedipus said a final farewell to his daughters, and asked them to stand aside so that he could say what Theseus alone might hear—instructions for the location of the grave that would guard the kingdom forever. Then, in an instant, Oedipus was gone—vanished, the Messenger says.

The tale told, the Messenger yields his place to Antigone and Ismene, who return weeping and grieving. They weep for their father, who has unaccountably disappeared, and they weep for themselves—young women with no home and no parents.

The Chorus empathizes with the women, but doesn't have much advice to offer. Once again, Theseus comes to their rescue. They beg him to show them where their father's tomb is, and he denies that request, but he promises to help them travel back home to Thebes. Antigone is desperate to stop the fratricide, and Theseus says he will do everything he can to help the women.

The play ends with the Chorus telling the women to stop weeping and grieving, because all things are in the hands of the gods.

Analysis

The speech by the Chorus that opens this section is another example of the weakness of this group. Commenting on the doom Polynices will face now, the Chorus takes a what-can-I-do? attitude, saying that all such things are left in the hands of the gods. The sudden rumblings of thunder underscore the point that the gods are mighty and these men are weak.

The play then moves very quickly to its conclusion. From the crashing, sizzling thunder and lightning bolts to the sudden disappearance of the body of Oedipus, the might and power of the gods are on full display.

The shattering fear that the display of thunder and lightning inspires in those who witness it can be seen as a warning to people who doubt the power of the gods. At the same time that the gods are rewarding Oedipus and redeeming his suffering, the divine powers of destruction are a not-so-subtle reminder of who's in charge.

It is a happy ending, of sorts. Oedipus finds his life redeemed, as he had been promised, and Theseus is given the great gift of eternal protection for Athens. The same divine power that visited destruction on Oedipus and his family now raises him up at the end of his life, showing that Olympian designs can take a whole human lifetime to unfold.

During the years when Sophocles lived, the popular culture contained rationalist attacks on the old gods and on the religion of the people who worshipped them, suggesting that some of the fierceness and glory with which Oedipus is punished and ultimately redeemed can be seen as commentary on real-life religious feuds.

Although the ending contains some redemption for Oedipus, his family's sufferings are not yet ended. Antigone and Ismene are adrift in a world where their only relatives are very unstable men. Their brothers are intent on mutual murder. Their uncle, Creon, has already shown that he cares less for them than for power.

Against this background, it seems foolhardy for Antigone to ask Theseus for help in getting back to Thebes. She intends to prevent the mutual slaughter of her brothers, she says. Theseus grants her request, and the wheels that move the machinery of her doom into place are already beginning to turn. Her story continues—and ends—in *Antigone*, the play that wraps up the remaining threads of the trilogy.

Study Questions

1. Why does Oedipus want Theseus summoned when the thunder peals?

2. How does the Chorus react to the thunder and lightning?

3. How does Theseus react to the weather?

4. What preparations does Oedipus ask his daughters to make?

5. Why does Oedipus whisper his final words to Theseus alone?

6. What does the Messenger see?

7. Why won't Theseus tell Antigone and Ismene where their father's tomb is?

8. Why does Antigone ask Theseus to help her and Ismene get back to Thebes?

9. Why does Theseus say that he will help the sisters?

10. What awaits the women in Thebes?

Answers

1. Oedipus wants Theseus summoned when the thunder peals because that is a sign from the gods that the end is near, and Oedipus wants to keep his promise to the king.

2. The Chorus reacts to the thunder and lightning with awe and prayers.

3. Theseus reacts to the weather by asking Oedipus what must be done.

4. Oedipus asks his daughters to gather water for him so that he may bathe and make an offering.

5. Oedipus whispers his final words to Theseus alone because only Theseus can know the location of the grave that will be the kingdom's strongest shield.

6. The Messenger sees Oedipus vanish.

7. Theseus won't tell Antigone and Ismene where their father's tomb is because the location must be kept secret.

8. Antigone asks Theseus to help her and Ismene get back to Thebes because she wants to prevent their brothers from killing each other.

9. Theseus says that he will help the sisters because it is his duty, which he must honor.

10. An uncertain fate awaits the women in Thebes. Their brothers are under a dreadful curse from their father, and their uncle, Creon, has already shown himself to be unstable and power-mad.

Suggested Essay Topics

1. The play ends with Oedipus giving Theseus his promised gift, and seemingly going to a peaceful and eternal rest. What kind of life do you think Oedipus will have in the kingdom of the dead?

2. Antigone and Ismene are bound for Thebes, where their brothers are bent on mutual murder and their uncle, Creon, sits on the throne. What prospects do you think await them back home?

3. Describe how the Chorus reacted to the Messenger's story. How would you have reacted to the tale if you lived in that time and place and shared the prevailing beliefs of the culture?

Antigone

Lines 1 – 376

New Characters:

Antigone: *the daughter of Oedipus and Jocasta, who are mother and son*

Ismene: *Antigone's sister*

Chorus: *a group of Theban elders and their leader, whose commentary helps the audience understand the events on stage*

Creon: *the King of Thebes, the uncle of Antigone and Ismene*

A Sentry: *a soldier*

Summary

The play opens when Eteocles and Polynices, the two sons of the ill-fated Oedipus and Jocasta, have just killed each other in battle. The two young men, Antigone's brothers, ended their lives fulfilling the curse called down on them by their father, when they denied him aid in his exile—to kill and be killed, brother by brother. The ancient audiences knew that these two deaths come on top of all the family's other tragedies.

The trouble between the two men began after Oedipus was driven into exile. Polynices claimed the throne, but his brother, Eteocles, fought him for it. Polynices lost, and departed for Argos, where he married. From there, he launched a war to win the crown of Thebes that he still thought was rightfully his. Eteocles stayed at

home with Creon, his uncle, who sits on the throne when the play begins. In a newly fought battle, with Polynices heading an army from Argos, and Eteocles fighting for Thebes, both brothers have just killed each other.

Antigone's first lines are a lament, heard by her sister, Ismene. "Our lives are pain," she says.

Creon, the king, is their uncle, and he has just made that pain even sharper, Antigone tells Ismene. Although the king will honor Eteocles with a military funeral, the king bars anyone from giving Polynices, the other brother, any burial rites. His corpse is to be left where it fell, to be food for vultures, Antigone says. Anyone who disobeys this order will be stoned to death.

Ismene is saddened by the news, but she feels that she can do nothing.

Antigone takes this decree as a challenge. Burial rituals were sacred obligations for Greek women, and she is willing to die to fulfill hers. Such a death will bring her everlasting praise among the gods and in the kingdom of the dead, she says. Frightened by Antigone's passion, Ismene rejects her sister's plea for help in honoring their brother. Reciting the tragedies that have already befallen the family—patricide, incest, suicide, fratricide—Ismene says that she and Antigone are too weak and alone to fight Creon's decree. "I must obey the ones that stand in power," Ismene says.

Antigone is insistent. Polynices must have a proper burial ceremony, and she is ready to die to give him one. If she is killed by the king, she will die knowing that she has served her brother, the gods and the kingdom of the dead, she says. Ismene promises to keep this plan secret, but Antigone says, "Tell the world."

The Chorus and their Leader come on-stage, to recount the battle. Creon comes on-stage, celebrating his victory and gloating over his now uncontested power. He announces that loyalty to the city—to him—must take precedence over all other loyalties.

Creon says that Polynices violated this loyalty by making war, and the traitor's corpse must therefore be left as carrion for birds and dogs. The Leader of the Chorus suggests that maybe this isn't such a good idea, and Creon gets indignant.

Then a Sentry enters. Breathless and frightened, he announces that someone has sprinkled dust on the corpse of Polynices and performed the proper funeral rites. Creon is furious. "What man alive would dare?" The Leader of the Chorus asks a question: "Could this possibly be the work of the gods?"

Creon flies into a rage. He denounces Polynices again as a traitor, and says that the gods take no interest in the dead man. In an instant, a conspiracy theory forms in his mind. Creon decides that the guards posted at the traitor's corpse have all been bribed and that the burial was their work. Frightened, the Sentry pleads innocence and leaves.

Analysis

Until now, Antigone has been at the mercy of events. Her family's disasters have been things that happened to her, not things in which she played an active role. But that is about to change. Antigone has decided that she will respond to the family's most recent tragedy—the mutual battlefield murders of her brothers, Eteocles and Polynices—by attempting to wrest from fate some portion of honor and glory for herself.

Antigone is ready to die to properly honor her dead brother, but Ismene doesn't think this is a good idea. Their lives are sad enough, Ismene says, what with having a father, Oedipus, who killed his own father and a mother who unknowingly married her own son. They don't need to risk certain death by defying Creon, their last male protector in a world where even women of royal blood are utterly dependent on the mercy of men.

Antigone answers by telling Ismene that she will do this deed alone. The two women part as loving sisters, having settled their differences with words. If only their brothers could have found peace that way, instead of resorting to mutual murder, Antigone would not be courting death now.

This section ends with a sentry informing Creon that someone, somehow, has defied the royal decree, slipped past the guards and administered the sacred funeral rites to Polynices.

When the Leader of the Chorus timidly suggests that this might be the work of the gods, it is implied that Creon's decree goes too far.

But Creon responds with a fit of paranoid rage, blaming the sentry and the rest of the troops posted near the corpse with conspiracy, betrayal and bribe-taking.

Creon and Antigone both presume to speak for the gods—Creon, when he says that the gods don't care about Polynices, and Antigone, when she says that she will find eternal honor if she defies Creon's decree.

It is clear that both Creon and Antigone justify their ideas and actions by claiming divine authority. The difference is that while Creon claims godly approval for deeds that further his selfish political ends, Antigone sees herself winning eternal honor and glory for a defiant act of sacrifice.

Study Questions

1. What are the family relationships of Antigone, Ismene, Polynices, Eteocles, Oedipus, Jocasta and Creon?

2. Why has Creon given an honorable burial to Eteocles but decreed that anyone doing the same for Polynices will be stoned to death?

3. How do Antigone and Ismene settle their differences?

4. What does Antigone say when Ismene promises to keep her secret?

5. What do we learn from the Chorus?

6. What is the underlying meaning of the speech the Leader of the Chorus delivers to Creon?

7. Why is the Sentry afraid to deliver his message?

8. How does Creon respond to the Sentry's message?

9. In her first speech, how does Antigone describe her life?

10. How does Ismene answer her sister?

Answers

1. Antigone and Ismene are sisters, and Polynices and Eteocles are their brothers. Creon is their maternal uncle. The brothers and sisters are the children of Oedipus and Jocasta, who were mother and son.

2. Creon gave an honorable burial to Eteocles but decreed anyone doing the same for Polynices will be stoned to death because Eteocles fought on Creon's side in battle. Polynices was in the enemy camp.

3. Antigone and Ismene settle their differences with words and part as loving sisters. Their brothers fight with swords and armies and commit mutual murder.

4. Antigone says she wants everyone to know that she intends to honor her brother and the gods by performing the sacred burial rites.

5. The Chorus tells us the details of the battle in which the brothers kill each other.

6. The leader of the Chorus suggests that Creon is drunk with power and revenge and that the gods might be appalled by his refusal of burial rites to his nephew.

7. The Sentry is afraid to deliver his message because Creon's rage is no secret.

8. Creon responds to the Sentry's message by voicing a paranoid conspiracy theory.

9. In her first speech, Antigone says that her life is pain.

10. Ismene answers her sister by saying that the immediate future could bring better luck or utter ruin.

Suggested Essay Topics

1. Until now, the many griefs of Antigone's life were mostly beyond her control. Ismene also suffered. The two women react in different ways to the news that Creon has barred anyone from administering burial rites their brother. Discuss the passions and fears that drive the sisters to their separate decisions.

2. Creon decreed that his nephew shall remain unburied because he was a traitor. There are clear hints that just as Antigone is courting death by her decision, Creon, too, flirts with doom. Discuss what happens when people pursue their own passions, regardless of the consequences.

3. Describe the family relationships between Antigone, Ismene, their brothers and Creon.

Lines 377 – 827

New Character:

Haemon: *the son of Creon, he is to be married to Antigone*

Summary

This section opens with a long speech by the Chorus that celebrates the powers of humanity but warns that justice and the gods are mightier.

After this meditation, Antigone enters, accompanied by a sentry. The Sentry immediately announces that she's been caught burying the body of Polynices, and asks for Creon. The king enters, and the Sentry proudly says that he's free and clear of this whole business, now that the prisoner has been caught giving funeral rites to Polynices. Astonished, the king demands details. The Sentry lays out the case against the prisoner. Furious now, the king dismisses the Sentry and confronts Antigone.

Proud and defiant, Antigone admits that she gave her brother burial rights and says she honors the laws of the gods above Creon's decree.

With this speech, Antigone gives a turn to the wheel of fate that has already carried her parents and her brothers to destruction. As they were unable to prevent tragedies from happening, so Antigone is rushing headlong toward doom.

The Leader of the Chorus observes that Antigone is as proud and wild as her father, and as certain to break rather than bend when trouble comes. Creon answers by promising to make an example of Antigone as a warning to anyone else considering defiance and treason.

The king confronts Ismene, who has been seized by guards and brought before him. At first, he wants to kill her along with Antigone. Ismene begs to die with her sister, but Antigone says that she prefers to die alone, having buried their brother alone. Ismene then pleads for her sister's life, reminding the king that his son is

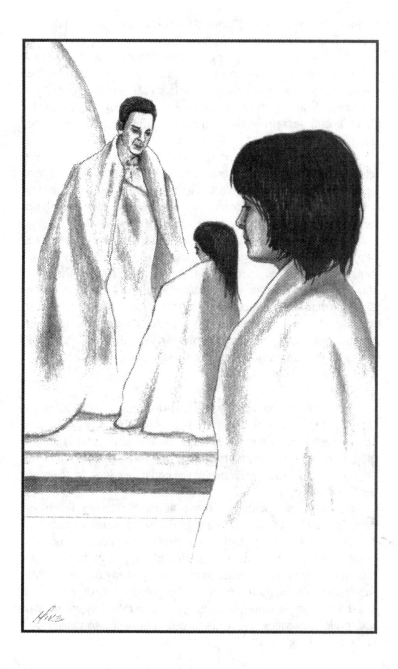

to marry Antigone. That attempt at stopping and changing fate only makes Creon more angry.

The Chorus speaks, giving a long meditation on how sorrow and destruction washes over many generations like the tide once the gods begin to wreck a family. The heirs of the house of Oedipus are being destroyed now by the same things that killed their father—bottomless pride, the vengeance of the gods and the fury of a raging heart.

Haemon, Creon's son enters, and the king gives the young man a lecture on love and marriage. Creon calls Antigone a traitor, and says she will find a husband among the dead. The king says that he must execute her as an example to the people he rules. He will not be defied, and he especially will not be defied by a woman, he says.

Haemon, who intends to marry Antigone, tells his father that the people in the streets are praising Antigone as a hero. People admire her courage and her commitment to her brother and the gods, Haemon says, and they will be more loyal to Creon if he spares Antigone than if he kills her. Blind determination and fury—the things that Creon sees in Antigone—will lead to the king's destruction, Haemon says. Creon rejects his son's advice. Disgusted, the young man says that Creon would make a fine king on a desert island.

Analysis

The opening speech by the Chorus sounds several major themes of the play—that human beings are immensely talented and powerful creatures who can harvest the earth's crops, sail the planet's oceans and tame its beasts. But when people reject the laws of the land and the justice of the gods, they face destruction, the Chorus says.

Not all human beings are brave, and some are too humble to commit the sin of hubris that brings down the House of Oedipus. The Sentry who brings Antigone to the palace as a prisoner is a coward, whose only concern is saving his own neck by finding a culprit for the king to punish. As the unwitting instrument of fate, the Sentry just wants to get in, get his job done and get out. He doesn't even know who Antigone is, and is completely unaware of the tragic consequences of his own urgent desire to get himself clear of the king's wrath.

This is an example of a theme that runs through the play—how people seem to fulfill what has been ordained by the gods simply by acting on impulse and instinct. If the Sentry had stopped for a moment to ask Antigone who she was or why she was doing what she was caught doing, he might have acted differently. But he didn't.

When she is presented to Creon, Antigone is so fiercely passionate about the glory she expects to win from the gods and the justice she thinks she has wrested from the king for her brother, it doesn't occur to her to ask for mercy.

It is possible that if Antigone tried to reason with Creon when he announced that anyone caught honoring Polynices with burial rites would be killed, she might have changed his mind and changed her fate. But she didn't try to persuade Creon to change his mind—she chose to act, instead.

Antigone's situation here is complex. She is presented as a person whose soul is caught in two conflicting but inextricably intertwined fates. One of her destinies is to carve out her own fate, which she does when she chooses to defy Creon. But it is also her destiny to continue the piling up of family tragedies that began before she was born. Like her Uncle Creon, and like her own dead parents, Antigone follows only her own passions, asking advice or help of no one. Like them, she will bring grief to others from the actions she chooses.

Ismene begs for her own death, but she also tries to break her family's fatal chain of tragedy, telling the king that he is robbing his son of a bride by killing Antigone. That plea is rejected, and Creon loses an opportunity to make fate change for the better.

Haemon echoes that advice when he tells his father that the people are crying for Antigone's freedom, and that the king can gain more authority by freeing Antigone than by killing her. Creon rejects his son's advice as he rejected Ismene's plea. Sorrowful and angry, the young man says that Creon would be a good king on a desert island, where his only subject would be himself.

The interactions of the main characters have built the philosophical framework for the main intellectual issues of the play: Is it fate that makes things happen in these people's lives? Is it the prophecies of the gods? Is it what's in their hearts and minds?

Study Questions

1. What is the purpose of the first long speech by the Chorus?

2. What does the Sentry see?

3. What is the Sentry's main concern?

4. Why does Creon intend to kill Ismene?

5. Why does Antigone reject Ismene by saying she prefers to die alone?

6. How does Ismene attempt to spare her sister's life?

7. What kind of a leader is Creon?

8. Who is Haemon?

9. What advice does Haemon give Creon?

10. How does Creon receive Haemon's advice?

Answers

1. The first long speech by the Chorus presents the audience with the intellectual issues that shape the play.

2. The Sentry sees the corpse of Polynices beginning to rot, and he and the other guards move it to higher ground on a bare, shelterless plain. While they are guarding the body, they see a dust storm so thick that the sky goes black even though the noontime sun was blazing overhead a moment ago. After the storm passes, the Sentry and the guards see a girl giving burial rites to Polynices.

3. The Sentry's main concern is clearing himself of Creon's suspicions and handing over the girl who was seen sanctifying the guarded corpse.

4. Creon intends to kill Ismene because he sees her as an accessory to Antigone's crime.

5. Antigone rejects Ismene by saying she prefers to die alone because she did the work of administering burial rites alone.

6. Ismene attempts to spare her sister's life by telling the king that an execution would deny his son a bride.

7. Creon leads by giving orders, not by listening. He demands complete loyalty, and punishes traitors with death.

8. Haemon is Creon's son, and he intends to marry Antigone.

9. Haemon tells Creon that leaders who hear the whispers and murmurs of their people are better kings than those who listen only to their own voices.

10. Creon receives Haemon's advice ungraciously, calling his son disobedient and rude for presuming to tell a king how to rule.

Suggested Essay Topics

1. Using examples of actions and their consequences from the play, discuss the role of fate in people's lives.

2. Antigone and Creon are uncle and niece, sharing some of the same blood. Yet he has condemned her to death. How do the ties of family weigh against the duties of a leader? Discuss this from Creon's point of view, from Antigone's and from Haemon's.

3. What are the obligations of the living to the dead? Discuss.

Lines 828 – 1,213

New Character:

Tiresias: *the blind prophet who sees the future*

Summary

Creon and Haemon argue bitterly over Antigone, and the young man accuses his father of profaning justice and the gods. The king is furious, and says that Haemon will never marry Antigone because she will soon be joining the dead. Haemon says that her death will kill another—a desperate proclamation of his love that Creon hears as a threat against the crown. In anger and sorrow, Haemon flees the palace.

The Leader of the Chorus asks Creon about Ismene and Antigone, and the king says that Ismene is, after all, innocent. But the king plans a living burial for Antigone in a tomb of rock. Commenting on what has happened so far, the Chorus speaks of love, and how its passion is fierce enough to destroy not only people but even the gods.

Antigone appears, and she knows that she has been sentenced to be buried alive. The Chorus comments on the unnaturalness of a vibrant young woman joining the kingdom of the dead while she is strong and well. Antigone compares her situation to that of Niobe, a woman part immortal and part mortal, whose arrogance the gods punished by turning her into stone that wept eternally.

The Chorus answers that comparison by saying that Antigone, although merely mortal, can no doubt comfort herself by seeing parallels between her life and the destiny of the gods. This sounds like an insult to Antigone, who lashes out at the Chorus. The Chorus responds by telling her that defying Creon was going too far, and asking if maybe this isn't the result of her father's crimes. Antigone says that maybe this is so. She recites all her family's tragic history. Creon says that she has nobody to blame but herself—that it was her decision to defy him and embrace death. He orders the guards to take her away and carry out his sentence.

On her way out, Antigone says that she looks forward to seeing her family in the kingdom of the dead. The underworld holds more joy and life for her now than the world of the living. She explains her actions to herself, saying that she would never have been driven to such a desperate end by the death of a child or a husband. Children die and parents have more. Husbands die and wives remarry. But with her mother and her father dead and her brothers following them, she is alone now and she can only join them.

The Leader of the Chorus observes that Antigone is still proud and defiant even as her own death approaches. The king orders her carried away. As she is led out under guard, the Chorus speaks. Piecing together mythology and history, they tell of Danae, who was imprisoned to prevent a prophecy from coming true. But she and her child, a son of Zeus, were spared, and fate intervened again later when Danae's son Perseus killed his grandfather, as prophesied. The Chorus describes all this by saying that nothing can change the power and force of fate. They tell other stories with similar conclusions—fate is everlasting and unchangeable.

Then the blind prophet, Tiresias, tells Creon his latest visions. The gods have been greatly offended by Creon's denial of a decent burial to Polynices, the prophet says. All manner of carrion eaters have been dragging chunks of flesh through the city, profaning the altars and hearths of the gods. In retaliation, the gods refuse the city's offerings. The birds whose cries the omen readers rely on are so gorged on the unclean flesh that they are useless as guides to the future. All of this will come to no good, Tiresias warns the king. Stubbornness and pride will be his downfall. The king rejects everything Tiresias has to say, and accuses him of attempting to extort money by planting fear.

Analysis

When the king and Haemon argue over Antigone, the young man attempts to change the fates of his beloved, his father and himself, but the king will not listen. People hear what they want to hear, and the king hears not love but treason. When Haemon says that Antigone's death will kill another, foreshadowing the prophecy Tiresias will soon make, an angry, paranoid and self-centered Creon assumes this to be a threat against him. Haemon flees, and fate marches on.

When the Chorus comments on the unnaturalness of Antigone joining the dead, they are developing a theme that runs through the play—that the gods expect human beings to honor a certain order of things and that violators will be punished. Creon violated that order when he forbade the gift of burial rites to Polynices, and he violates it again when he orders Antigone's death. Her parents have violated it in multiple ways, and their lives were accordingly tragic.

By invoking Niobe and Danae in her speeches, Antigone is linking herself to the shared cultural and religious history of the audience. Niobe insulted and angered the gods with her arrogance, and spending eternity drenching her stone body with a rivulet of tears was her punishment. Danae, the mother of the hero Perseus, was fated to play a part in an inter-generation tragedy not so different from the drama enacted by Antigone's parents. Despite years of attempts to block fate, Danae's son eventually killed his grandfather, as foretold.

The storytelling traditions of the ancient world featured many complex interactions between gods and mortals, with consequences that spanned several generations. Those secular and religious stories, like the history of the House of Oedipus, often featured the fulfillment of grim prophecies by people trying urgently to avoid them.

The blind prophet, Tiresias, offers Creon a chance to escape the cruel embrace of fate, but the king rejects everything Tiresias says. Fate will continue to have its way with these characters.

Study Questions

1. What threat does Haemon make?

2. How does the king interpret Haemon's threat?

3. Whose fate does Antigone say is similar to her own?

4. How does the Chorus respond when Antigone compares her fate to the destiny of a women—Niobe —with immortal blood?

5. Why does Tiresias come to the palace?

6. What goes wrong with the omens and the offerings?

7. How have the altars been profaned?

8. How does Creon dismiss the prophecies Tiresias offers?

9. What is the most dreadful thing Tiresias says?

10. How do the masses feel about Creon according to Tiresias?

Answers

1. Haemon warns the king that there will be another death if Antigone is executed.

2. The king interprets this as a threat on his life.

3. Antigone says that the fate of Niobe is similar to her own. Niobe was from a family whose tragedies and glories were in many ways similar to those of the House of Oedipus. Grief-stricken after she and her family are punished by the gods, Niobe is turned to stone and her tears run forever down the hard surface that once was flesh.

4. When Antigone compares her fate to Niobe's, the Chorus says that she is taking comfort from comparing herself, a mere mortal, to someone who is descended from gods.

5. Tiresias comes to the palace to tell Creon that things are terribly wrong. He has long given the king advice, and feels it is his duty to do so again.

6. The gods will not accept the offerings, and the birds who speak omens are too gorged on carrion to share their knowledge.

7. The altars been profaned by scavenger beasts dragging bits of unburied flesh around the city.

8. Creon dismisses the prophecies Tiresias offers by accusing him of hoping to reap money by planting fear.

9. The most dreadful thing Tiresias says is that Creon's decision to kill Antigone will cost the king a child of his own.

10. According to Tiresias, the masses now hate their king.

Suggested Essay Topics

1. Find a good anthology of stories about the gods and goddesses worshipped by the ancient Greeks, and compare and contrast the family stories of Niobe and Danae with what you know so far about Antigone and her family.

2. Write about an example in the life of someone you know where a willingness to listen made everything turn out better than it otherwise might have.

3. Pick an example from the play of an action whose consequences are unintended and unexpected. Discuss.

Lines 1,214 – 1,470

New Characters:

A Messenger: *a man who delivers news*

Eurydice: *the wife of King Creon, the mother of Haemon*

Summary

When the Leader of the Chorus tells Creon that Tiresias has always been a truthful man, the king agrees. Suddenly confessing himself to be shaken and torn by the blind old man's warning, Creon asks for advice. The Leader of the Chorus tells Creon to free Antigone from her walled burial vault and to build a proper tomb for her brother. Creon says he will do these things.

The Chorus speaks now, invoking the god Dionysus and preparing for festivities in his name. Creon has repented his wrath and his decree, the natural order of things is to be restored, and there is general rejoicing. The Chorus has spoken too soon. The tragedies that began taking root when Creon decreed that Antigone must die are beginning to flower now.

First, a Messenger delivers horrible news. Haemon has run himself through with his own sword, in grief over his lost love. The Leader of the Chorus interrupts this report to say that Tiresias was right, and to suggest that the worst is yet to come.

Eurydice, the king's wife and Haemon's mother, overhears the Messenger's news and asks for all the details. Obliging her, the Messenger relates how he and the king set out to right everything that was wrong—to give Polynices a final, proper burial and to free Antigone from the living death to which she was sentenced.

After they honor Polynices, they make their way to Antigone. They hear a far-off, grief-stricken wailing and Creon recognizes Haemon's voice. The king's party runs ahead and discovers a tragedy. Antigone has committed suicide—choosing to die quickly by her own hand rather than slowly by starvation in her tomb. Haemon was first to discover her. When the king and his party reach him, he is holding her and grieving.

Creon pleads with Haemon to leave, and the young man lunges at his father, sword in hand. He misses his father but buries the

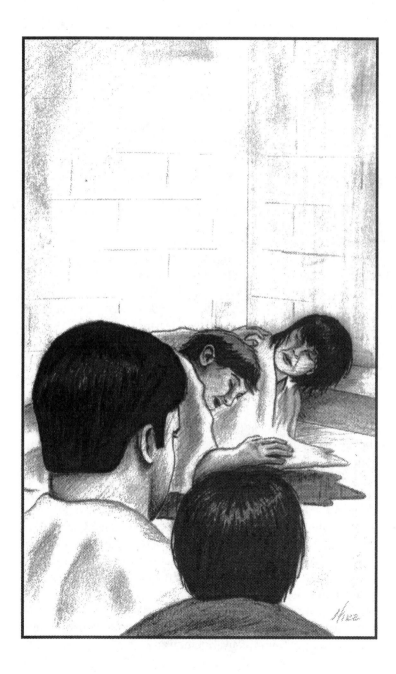

sword in his own body. Haemon breathes his last, embracing Antigone a final time.

Hearing this, Eurydice turns and leaves the messenger. A moment later, Creon accompanies his dead son's body across the stage. Now, when it is too late for the king to prevent the tragedies he set in motion, he understands the consequences of his actions. He apologizes to the Chorus for his crimes, his stupidity and his fanaticism. He says that he is made wise now by blood and tears.

The final tragedy of this play is announced by the Messenger—Eurydice is a suicide, too, and she dies cursing her husband. Distraught and desperate, Creon assumes the blame and says that death is all he has to look forward to now.

The Leader suggests that Creon's doom and salvation come from the future—his doom because he ignored it when he sentenced Antigone to death and his salvation because he might yet be able to redeem himself by thinking of it now.

The play ends with a simple statement from the Chorus. Proud people are inevitably humbled by fate, and fate will in the end teach them what they otherwise could not learn.

Analysis

Frightened by Tiresias, the king realizes that he may well have set in motion a chain reaction of tragedies worse than anything he intended. Fate unfolds in ways that mere mortals cannot predict. The overall design is impossible for human beings to discern when their actions knit the first stitches, but the pattern becomes visible soon enough.

Now that he sees some of the consequences of his deeds, Creon is frantic to undo what he has done. He says he will see to a proper burial for Polynices and that he will free Antigone.

The Chorus is happy that fate seems to have been steered from tragedy to joy, and speaks of celebrations. Unfortunately, this happiness turns out to be premature. What is done is done and cannot be undone, and the remainder of the play reinforces that idea with ever-increasing momentum.

The history of the House of Oedipus is the story of great passion fated to come to great grief, and this play ends with three consecutive suicides—Antigone, Haemon and Eurydice—that share a grim inevitability.

When she is walled into her burial vault with nothing but her thoughts of eternal honor and glory for company, Antigone decides that the world of the living holds nothing for her and she chooses to die quickly rather than slowly. The fierce, mad grief of her decision has its own internal logic—Antigone is carrying out the last act of a family tragedy that began with the sad prophecies preceding her father's birth.

Just as her parents scorned and mocked the gods by proclaiming their desires to thwart fate, so Antigone hastens her own destruction. If she had only been a little less certain of the righteousness of her cause and a little less anxious to embrace death, she could have spared herself a death sentence in the first place. Having earned that death sentence, she might have enjoyed the benefits of Creon's change of heart if she hadn't been so eager to visit the kingdom of the dead.

Antigone's body is cold and her spirit is gone when Haemon comes to her tomb, and the arc of the play's grief-driven logic continues on course. As fiercely passionate as his dead true love, Haemon can only follow her to the kingdom of the dead. The play's arc of grief then reaches to Haemon's mother, who decides to follow her son to death, cursing her husband with her last breath. By now, Creon is a shattered man who says he understands that he is the cause of all these deaths and this misery. He has come to this pass because he neglected the future in the past, the Leader of the Chorus tells him. If he is to redeem himself at all, he must think of the future now.

The play ends with a simple statement from the Chorus that is a constant theme in much of ancient Greek literature. Unless checked with wisdom, kindness and good judgment, great leaders will be destroyed by fate, which is mightier even than they are. The humility that some people learn the easy way sometimes has to be learned by the mighty in the most difficult way.

Antigone stands as one of the most powerful dramas handed down to us by the ancient world because its themes still speak to us today. The eternal conflicts between free will and fate, human independence and family history, the divine and secular worlds and doom and redemption are as real now as they were then.

Study Questions

1. What does Creon fear will happen to him if he heeds the advice Tiresias has given?

2. What does Creon admit after he decides to take the prophet's advice?

3. Where does Antigone die?

4. Why does Haemon kill himself?

5. How does Haemon's mother, Eurydice, hear of his death?

6. What does Eurydice do after Haemon's death?

7. How does Creon discover Haemon's death?

8. When does Creon discover his wife's death?

9. How does Creon react to all these tragedies?

10. Chorus sums up the preceeding events in what manner?

Answers

1. Creon fears that he will lose his pride if he heeds the advice Tiresias has given him.

2. After he decides to take the prophet's advice, Creon admits that he is afraid.

3. Antigone hangs herself in the tomb in which she was buried alive, choosing a quick death over a slow one.

4. After he discovers Antigone's death, Haemon falls on his sword.

5. Haemon's mother, Eurydice, learns that he has killed himself when she overhears the Messenger giving the Chorus the news.

6. Eurydice reacts to Haemon's death calmly at first, then she kills herself.

7. Creon is there when Haemon kills himself. Attempting to undo the chain of tragedies that he has set in motion, Creon goes to Antigone's tomb to free her, only to discover her suicide and to witness his son's death.

8. Creon discover his wife's death when a Messenger brings him the news.

9. Creon reacts to all these tragedies by admitting that his rashness caused them.

10. The Chorus sums the preceeding events with a meditation on the idea that the mightiest people sometimes learn what they need to know only in the wake of great tragedies.

Suggested Essay Topics

1. A modern-day variation on the ancient Greek theme of great leaders being brought low as a consequence of their hubris is the saying that "Pride goeth before a fall." Discuss three examples of this theme from modern times.

2. The play ends with all the major characters except Creon dead by their own hands. Although he is the force who set all these deaths into motion, he is the only one who survives. Discuss this in terms of the burden that Creon will bear in this life and in the next.

3. Antigone vowed to bury her brother in accordance with the funeral rites of her religion, and she knew that she was risking her life to do it. She was certain that the gods would honor her for her sacrifice. Discuss the cultural implications of believing that there is divine reward for sacrificing your life to serve the gods. Compare this with a belief system that says that human life is precious and that reasonable and kind gods should not expect people to sacrifice their lives for rewards to be obtained in the kingdom of the dead.

Sample Analytical Paper Topics

The three plays known as the *Oedipus Trilogy* can be studied separately or together, depending on the goals and ambitions of the class. Using the following outlines, develop and write papers on one, two or all three of the plays.

Topic #1

Loyalty to family members is a major theme in the *Oedipus Trilogy*. Discuss the importance of kinship.

Outline

I. Thesis Statement: *The obligations of kinship are a major theme throughout these plays. The characters honor the demands of kinship above everything else, with no concern about the repercussions.*

    A. Antigone is willing to give her life to bury her brother properly.

    B. Antigone follows her father into exile as his companion and his guide.

II. Loyalty to kinship has varying results.

    A. Antigone is sentenced to death by Creon, her uncle, who angers the gods.

    B. Antigone is honored and loved by her father, and she earns his gratitude.

III. Conclusion: Kinship obligations were life and death matters for the Greeks.

  A. Antigone hastens her death sentence by committing suicide. Haemon, her would-be groom, finds her body and kills himself so that they can be reunited in the kingdom of the dead.

   1. Haemon's father must bear the burden of knowing that he is responsible for the deaths of two young people.

   2. Creon's queen, Haemon's mother, kills herself when she hears that her son is dead. Her blood also stains Creon's hands.

  B. Antigone and Ismene are faithful to their obligations to their father, but their brothers ignore him in exile.

   1. The brothers are punished with their father's curse, which they fulfill by killing each other in battle.

  C. The gods reward Oedipus for his suffering. Although he committed crimes against his parents, he acted unknowingly. He took good care of his children, asking Creon to watch the girls when he was banished. The gods weighed his good deeds against his crimes and found that he fulfilled his kinship obligations when they weren't hidden from him by fate.

Topic #2

Many characters in the *Oedipus Trilogy* have power. Discuss how different characters use their power, giving examples from the plays.

Outline

I. Thesis statement: *One of the main themes of the plays is the use and abuse of power. Power can be used for destruction, or it can be used to achieve greatness.*

  A. Examples of the uses and abuses of power.

    1.   Theseus, in *Oedipus at Colonus*, is a kind and just king who is modest about his victories in battle, faithful to his promises, and willing to do the right thing.

    2.   Creon, in *Oedipus at Colonus*, and in *Antigone* is a vain and crude man who acts on whims, and destroys people weaker than he is.

II. Sometimes the people who are the least powerful turn out to be the mightiest shapers of human destiny and fate.

    A. Give examples of minor characters shaping major events.

       1.   In *Oedipus the King*, a Messenger from Corinth casually remarks that Oedipus was only the adopted son of the royal couple who raised him, unleashing the rest of the play's grief.

       2.   In *Oedipus the King*, Tiresias sees the future and tries to prevent the truth from being revealed.

III. Conclusion: Power can be used for good or evil.

    A. Give examples from the plays supporting this conclusion.

       1.   Creon is a bad king; he sentences Antigone to death and refuses her brother a proper burial.

       2.   Theseus is good and just; he offers Oedipus protection in his time of need.

Topic #3

In Sophocles' time, the Gods determined a person's fate. This fate was unalterable, despite all attempts to do so.

Outline

I. Thesis Statement: *Fate is an unalterable force in the lives of the characters in the the plays. Characters who attempt to thwart fate fail, despite their good intentions.*

    A. Jocasta and Laius attempt to alter the prophecies of the Gods.

       1.   Jocasta and Laius abandon their infant son, Oedipus, on a mountain in an effort to thwart fate.

2. Jocasta implores Oedipus not to investigate the murder of the Laius.

B. Oedipus tries to avoid his destiny.

1. Oedipus flees his home.

2. He marries the widowed Queen Jocasta, a stranger.

II. When people attempt to thwart fate and celebrate their triumph over the gods, they will be punished by the gods.

A. Examples of this divine retribution.

1. Creon sentencing Antigone to death, in violation of the laws of the kingdoms of the dead and of the living, suffers the suicide of his son and wife.

2. Creon, using force to gain power, is hated by his subjects, and lives a miserable life alone.

B. Examples of how people cope with divine retribution.

1. In *Oedipus at Colonus,* Oedipus says that he realizes that he had to be punished for his crimes but maintains that he acted as the pawn of the gods. He accepts his punishment but proclaims his innocence.

2. Oedipus is content, knowing his burial site will be sacred.

III. Conclusion: Fate is a force that cannot be altered, despite all attempts to do so.

A. Examples from the plays.

1. Jocasta, Laius, and Oedipus all try to avert the prophecies of the Gods throughout *Oedipus.* They are thwarted at each attempt.

2. Antigone and Ismene attempt to prevent their brothers from killing each other in battle, they too, fail.

3. Ismene tries to prevent another tragedy by appealing to Creon to free Antigone. Creon attempts to, but is too late.

SECTION SIX

Bibliography

Edition of the Play Used:

Sophocles, *The Three Theban Plays.* Translated by Robert Fagles, New York: Penguin Books USA, 1984.

Reference Materials:

Hamilton, Edith, *The Greek Way.* New York: Random House, 1942.

Knox, Bernard, *Oedipus at Thebes, Sophocles' Tragic Hero and His Time.* New Haven: Yale University Press, 1966.